I hope you get a
and you master your craft.
You are capable of achieving
any goal you set yourself
I miss you and I hope to
see you soon.   Arturo

Monologues for Kids and Tweens

100 Original Comedy and Drama Monologues for Young Actors

Visualize the
future you want
and live it.

Dawg.

Monologues for Kids and Tweens

100 Original Comedy and Drama Monologues for Young Actors

Mike Kimmel

Foreword by Sharon Garrison

ISBN 10: 0998151327
ISBN 13: 9780998151328

Ben Rose Creative Arts
New York - Los Angeles

Printed in the United States of America
First Edition

Publisher's Cataloging-in-Publication Data
provided by Five Rainbows Cataloging Services

Names: Kimmel, Mike, author. | Garrison, Sharon, writer of
foreword.
Title: Monologues for kids and tweens : 100 original comedy and
drama monologues for young actors / Mike Kimmel ; foreword
by Sharon Garrison.
Description: First edition. | Los Angeles : Ben Rose Creative Arts,
2019. | Grades 2-8.
Identifiers: ISBN 978-0-9981513-2-8 (paperback) | ISBN 978-0-
9981513-3-5 (EPUB ebook) | ISBN 978-0-9981513-4-2
(MOBI ebook)
Subjects: LCSH: Monologues–Juvenile literature. | Acting–
Auditions-Juvenile literature. | Comedy–Juvenile literature. |
Drama–Juvenile literature. | BISAC: JUVENILE NONFICTION /
Performing Arts / General. | YOUNG ADULT NONFICTION /
Performing Arts / General. | PERFORMING ARTS / Monologues
& Scenes. | PERFORMING ARTS / Acting & Auditioning.
Classification: LCC PN2080 .K56 2019 (print) | LCC PN2080
(ebook) | DDC 812/.6–dc23.

Interior design by Booknook.biz.

Praise for
Monologues for Kids and Tweens

"Well done, Mike! These monologues for young actors are funny, touching, accessible and great teaching tools not only for acting but for life."

> – Emily Mann
> Artistic Director and Resident Playwright
> McCarter Theatre Center
> National Theatre Conference Person of the Year, 2011

"Mike's latest book is a must have for kids and tweens who are even thinking about acting and auditioning. The monologues are brilliant! And the best part, there's one to fit every audition, no matter what. An incredible variety of monologues that highlight each human emotion ... funny, heartwarming, personal ... you name it, it's in this book! Mike's done it again, he's created another excellent guide to help young actors master their craft."

> – Suzanne Lyons
> Producer, Snowfall Films, Inc.
> *Undertaking Betty, The Calling, Jericho Mansions, Bailey's Billions, Portal, Seance, The Chaperone, Candy Stripers*

"Mike's monologues for kids are refreshing and fun. As an acting coach, I'm pleased to have this material for my students. Mike has a real gift for writing while keeping his monologues concise and memorable."

– Will Wallace
Director, Producer, Actor, and Acting Coach
The Will Wallace Acting Company
The Thin Red line, I Am Sam, Trafficked, Beverly Hills 90210, The Great Race, Warning Shot, The Tree of Life

"Mike Kimmel has crafted fun and creative monologues for the young actor. There are monologues in Mike's book that are filled with reflective, lightly comical, yet teaching moments lifted for the thoughts of the young. It makes for a nice addition to any young actor's 'tool box.'"

– Nicole Connor
Talent Agent, Youth Department
Central Artists Talent Agency

"Finally, a monologue book that is introspective and yet able to be expressed believably through the voice of a child. It's refreshing to see dialogue that makes our young performers sound confident and intelligent for their age and not just pandering to the latest social agenda. Thank you, Mike, for creating a clean set of entertaining monologues!"

– GiGi Erneta
Actress, Radio and TV Host and Writer
Flag of My Father, When the Bough Breaks, Risen, Nashville, The First, Jane the Virgin, Veep, Scandal, American Crime, Queen of the South, Body Cam, NCIS New Orleans, Dallas, Friday Night Lights, Veronica Mars

"Mike Kimmel has done it again. He has beautifully crafted a series of *Monologues for Kids and Tweens*. Poignant little observations of life that a young person can relate to and thus give a good performance and garner confidence and grow as an artist. These monologues are wonderful observations of life and humor, subtle humor, and some great life truths."

– Susannah Devereux
Actor, *Iron Thunder, Jimmy Zip, Chasing Ghosts, Chronology, Fogg, Silver Twins, Those People, Opposite of Earnest*
Portrayed Diane Neilson in *Shortland Street,*
    South Pacific Pictures for Television New Zealand

"In this book, Kimmel has crafted a great selection of pieces varying in tone and subject that are perfect for the young performer. When I work with children, I often seek out material that allows for us to really delve into character exploration and storytelling. For this process, it's so refreshing to have a compilation of monologues that support good values and personal growth for the child's development, both as an actor and as an empathetic human being."

"*Monologues for Kids and Tweens* is a fantastic book for the young aspiring actor. Each monologue is short and smart, with fun word play and a great attitude. These are monologues that will stick with you long after the audition – and remind you that keeping a smile on your face is the best way to go through life."

"Mike Kimmel is a monumentally talented artist. This book is a go-to book for those dabbling in the art of acting. It's the perfect way to fortify your craft and become successful in the daunting world of show business. Mike Kimmel was a tremendous mentor to me during my successful career in the Big Apple."

"Mighty Mike Kimmel has done it again with *Monologues for Kids and Tweens*. The monologues are not only suitable and timely for modern day kids and tweens, some are positive and uplifting. We all need that at any age. Mighty Mike delivers. Take it from a guy who knows from experience, Mike is as fun to read as he is on a TV or movie set!"

"Mike's latest book is a collection of monologues that are not only fun to learn, rehearse, and use, but heartfelt and thought-provoking. He's incorporated life lessons into scenarios that provide young actors with opportunities to rehearse all aspects of their skills including speech and voice, movement, and emotion. I highly recommend this book!"

–Tina Guillot
Toastmasters International District Director 2016-2017
John Maxwell Certified Coach, Trainer, and Speaker
Contributing Author,
101 Great Ways to Compete in Today's Job Market

"These short pieces acknowledge – and rightly so – that kids live in imperfect families in an imperfect world. They touch on loss ("The Comfy Red Chair"), consequences ("Green Bananas"), shame ("Little People"), duty ("New Old Sneakers"), nostalgia ("Little Magic Donut Seeds," "Ginger Ale is Good For You") ... a variety of struggles relatable to kids and adults alike. The word that comes to mind is humanism. Each monologue, in its own way, asks the same question: what kind of person do you want to be? Each invites kids to choose a positive frame of mind. Recurring themes include free agency and the innate goodness of humankind. What an uplifting message for kids and tweens! It's a good dose of cheer for adults as well. Oh, and I have become a better driver thanks to 'The Almost Stop Sign.'"

– Eva C. Nusbaum
Two-Time President
New Orleans Toastmasters

"Mike Kimmel is a phenomenal writer! Kimmel's witty comedy mixed with his awesome real-life approach with *Monologues for Kids and Tweens* – I've never seen it done! This book is for every aspiring young actor! It also allows kids and tweens to feel connected to the industry, and allows them to develop their own style of acting! This book is timeless and will remain current as any fashion trend!"

– Sonthia Coleman, MBA
The Fashion Brand Guru
Fashion Brand Strategist and Merchandiser

"Finding a quality monologue can be a challenging task when looking for something original and not heard many times over. In addition, finding something appropriate for a kid or tween takes even more of an effort. The monologues in Mike Kimmel's book I have found to be very interesting and even provide insight and perspective ... sometimes a very unique perspective. Not only does he provide stories that are fun to share, but some are geared at taking you from a negative to a positive mindset and, at times, include a few helpful life tips. I feel these are all very important concepts for kids and tweens who may also gain some insight while performing an entertaining and, at times, very funny monologue. This is a win-win for all. I mean, honestly, if they get lost in the story or you make them laugh, you WILL be remembered."

– Gwendolynn Murphy
Dallas Mavericks Dancers Alumni
Theater, TV and Film Actress,
The Harrowing, Baba Yaga, Glow, Hiding In Plain Sight,
The Deep End, Kung Fu Girls Club, Walker, Texas Ranger,
Murder Made Me Famous

"I love that Mike is continuing with this series. There just aren't enough CURRENT texts for kids to use. Whether it be for class, public speaking, or auditions, *Monologues for Kids & Tweens* will be a welcome addition to any library's Juvie collection."

— Danica Sheridan
Young Adult Librarian
American Library Association's
Young Adult Library Association (YALSA)
Actor, *Nip/Tuck, The Great Buck Howard, Scrubs, Everybody Hates Chris, Will & Grace, Phat Girlz, Angel, Alex & Emma, Judging Amy, Married with Children*

For David, Gabriel, Elianna, and Michael,
who inspire me across a mighty ocean

"I'm a success today because I had a friend who believed in me and I didn't have the heart to let him down."

– Abraham Lincoln

Table of Contents

Longer Scenes for Advanced Students

Foreword

Almost all kids crave attention. They will sing and dance, do head and handstands, wear silly costumes, and recite poems and nursery rhymes – giggling in pure delight for their attentive audiences. Occasionally, a child stands out from the crowd in a rather remarkable way, and we witness a talent emerging with that raw, unabashed and unapologetic delivery usually found only in a very young actor. Older actors tend to spend their whole lives struggling through acting classes and coaching sessions in an attempt to regain that perfect, simplistic exuberance they had as children.

What are the tools and support systems that actors, both young and old, must have to train and thrive? How do we identify them and how do we know what works? Has the availability of these resources evolved over the years? Are these developing materials of the highest quality actors need?

I am an actor. I was born an actor (so my parents always said) and will always be an actor. My journey is not unique. After appearing on live television when I was five, I was hooked. Once bitten by the acting bug, I sought every opportunity to entertain anyone who would watch and respond – with applause, of course! However, there I was, a youngster without access to drama or acting classes in my hometown. This fact resulted in me becoming very creative in finding chances to perform: variety shows on my front porch; plays I wrote, directed and starred in with my brother and patient cousins. (We filmed them on an 8mm silent camera.) Why was acting so essential to me? I've often wondered what crept into my DNA that made creating characters and performing them as much a part of my existence as breathing. Can't explain it, so I may as well just go with it.

Thankfully, over the past few decades, I have witnessed an exponential increase in accessible opportunities for young actors to practice and learn the acting skills needed to be successful. I find that most cities and towns proudly boast one or more community theaters, professional theaters and a drama school or two. What a wonderful thing that is for those of us who love the performing arts.

The actor I am today is the result of a long journey beginning with endless dance and voice lessons; intense training with acting coaches; college degrees in theatre, television and communications; successes as well as failures; and most important of all, the good counsel and support of so many peers and mentors. It just so happens that one of those mentors is my good friend, trusted colleague and author of this book, Mike Kimmel. It wasn't so long ago that Mike seized the opportunity to inspire and encourage me during a low point in my journey. "Trust yourself, your training, your instincts and your talent," he told me. He challenged me to step outside my comfort zone, travel out of state to pursue new audition opportunities in neighboring markets – and shoot for the moon! Since those collaborative days, my television, commercial and film career blossomed beyond expectations, and Mike became a successful author with a unique talent to speak eloquently from a child's point of view.

As I write this foreword, you should know that my favorite occupation outside of performing proved to be teaching drama. Working with young actors to develop their individual talents allowed me to fulfill a passion that I sensed as far back as I can remember. Also, in my thirty-plus years of teaching, my specialty field was always drama training for younger actors ages six through twelve. What a blessing to have enjoyed so many opportunities to blend my acting career with my love of teaching.

Not too long ago, Mike and I were discussing new opportunities for him to write his original musings for children. During that chat, I reiterated the difficulty I had experienced finding written texts, especially monologues, that could interest and inspire my kiddos without talking down to them. Mike embraced the challenge! With so many years of experience in developing drama curricula for young actors, I am enthusiastic and qualified to discuss the continuing need for meaningful and appealing dramatic material for children.

The quest for such material is now a lot easier. With his fourth and latest book, *Monologues for Kids and Tweens*, Mike Kimmel has once again created a wealth of inspirational and effective study and performance tools. This collection of charming, often soul-searching and age appropriate monologues provides a much-needed resource for budding young performers. To the teachers, coaches, agents and parents who use this collection: you can trust and feel confident with these tools. To you kids: read, study, prepare and be inspired by this outstanding resource now available for practice, auditions, classwork ... and just plain fun!

And last of all, to the amazing Mighty Mike: I continue to cherish your warmth, wisdom and inspiration as a friend and mentor. And now I am also grateful for these original little gems that you created for our youngest actors, providing them with effective tools that will help launch their own journeys into this wonderful world of make-believe.

Sharon Garrison
Dallas, Texas

Acknowledgments

As always, a million thanks to Mollie, Adele, and Tammy, my three incredible sisters. Their kindness, graciousness, and generosity are truly limitless. More importantly, they never gave up on their weird little brother – or laughed at his big, bold Hollywood dreams.

Many thanks to Kimberly Bliquez, GiGi Erneta, Tina Guillot, Roxanne Hernandez, Misty Marshall, Eva Nusbaum, Karen Pavlick, Jan Sutton, Rhae Ann Theriault, Marlene Wieden, Stephen Bowling, David Breland, Francis Ford Coppola, Sammy and Jennifer Maloof, Ben McCain, Jim and Angela O'Doherty, Morgan Roberts, and Ben Rose for their encouragement, support, inspiration, and unwavering loyalty.

Very special thanks to my dear friend Sharon Garrison for sharing her unique insights as both a teacher and performer in the foreword to this book. Sharon is a brilliant, dynamic force of nature – on stage, on screen, and in life.

Introduction

It's been said that adults are simply children who have become obsolete. "Do not grow old," Albert Einstein warned us, "no matter how long you live. Never cease to stand like curious children before the Great Mystery into which we were born." That's brilliant advice from one of the greatest thinkers of all time. A child's honest perspective gives adults a rare glimpse inside the youthful mind – and reminds us of the rich, active imagination children possess. It's a vibrant, optimistic, creative way of looking at the world that most adults, unfortunately, have long since relinquished. These qualities make children particularly well suited for actor training on stage and screen.

If you're a young person interested in acting, I'm honored and delighted you selected this book to help develop your skills, practice your technique, and perform your monologues. Thank you. Your willingness to read, study, and learn shows discipline, focus, and respect for the art, craft, and business of acting. Those are exceptional qualities to find in a young person's character. I know they will benefit you in all areas of your life and work.

If you're a parent, family member, teacher, or acting coach, I hope you will find these monologues useful and enjoyable for your youngsters. There is a wide variety of material to choose from, ranging from silly to serious, and short to long. I believe you will find an appropriate script in this collection to suit the temperament and interests of the young actors in your life. I thank you – and applaud you – for taking the time and initiative to assist them in this journey.

Let me share a secret about show business. Nobody ever really fails as an actor. The vast majority of actors, however, quit trying much too soon. That's the big, ugly secret. Show business is an extremely competitive field for actors of every age – including children. As a result, many people pursue acting for a little while – and then give up on their show business dreams once they hit the first big bump in the road. When they don't see positive results materializing as quickly as they hoped and expected, many wonderful actors quit the business and move on to something else. I've seen it happen hundreds of times. Maybe even thousands of times.

One of my great heroes is Benjamin Disraeli, who was Prime Minister of England more than a hundred years ago. "The secret to success," Disraeli told us, "is constancy of purpose." That's just as true today as it was back in the 1800s. We must keep going. We must be willing to hammer away relentlessly at our goals. We must be willing to work longer, harder, and smarter than our family, friends, and teachers think we can.

Acting on stage and screen is not nearly as easy as it looks. It looks easy when we see people doing it well. But people who do it well have been studying, practicing, and developing their craft for a very long time. Many people start out with a great deal of talent and natural ability. It takes patience, dedication, and commitment, however, to turn that raw talent into a reliable technique we can duplicate at will – and use to solid advantage every time we step into an audition room.

One of the most important skills young actors need to acquire is the ability to speak realistically and conversationally to scene partners and audiences. Realism is always the goal. This is true when working with both comedic and dramatic material. Ideally, actors should also strive to become equally comfortable performing both comedy and drama scripts.

Realism and a natural, conversational speaking style are vitally important in performing both scenes and monologues. Monologues offer a terrific opportunity to develop skill and confidence in all areas of the performing arts – and in many other areas of our lives. Actors often wonder why agents and casting directors ask them to perform monologues. There's an excellent reason. Monologues allow industry professionals to see how well actors can communicate material they select, memorize, and practice on their own. An actor's *choice of monologue* also provides clues into his or her unique character and personality.

In this book, young actors will find a variety of monologues on subjects easily relatable to their real-life roles as students, daughters, sons, and siblings. Several of the monologues offer advice on study skills, getting along well with others at home and school, and making lemonade when life throws lemons at us. There are positive messages and life lessons sprinkled throughout, as well. Most actors, I've found, respond extremely well to a strategically placed encouraging word.

Additionally, monologues in which kids and tweens address grown-up topics are particularly interesting for industry professionals. Besides standard childhood topics like homework, school, and family, it's fascinating for talent agents, casting directors,

directors, and producers to watch young actors tackle the very same subjects with which adults themselves commonly struggle.

Of course, children of six, eight, or even ten years of age haven't had direct experience with marriage, divorce, driving, getting a job, running a marathon, or any of the other grown-up topics in this book. Indirect experience in these areas, however, can be powerful and enlightening. Children can certainly observe and comment upon their parents' and older family members' experiences. In this way, children provide a marvelous youthful perspective on these diverse – and often confounding – adult topics. A child's thoughts – voiced out loud, as if the youth is speaking to himself or herself in private – provide fertile ground for solo audition pieces. A child's unique perspective and curiosity regarding the complexities of the adult world offers strong, dynamic material for monologues.

The monologues in this book are intended to give young performers fresh scenarios to explore, as well as greater depth and variety in their audition choices. Adult questions and settings may previously have been outside children's range of experience – and outside their comfort zones, as well. Stepping outside our comfort zones, however, needs to become standard practice for actors. We must always stretch ourselves as artists. That's how we learn where our limits are – and how we learn to move past them.

Here's a suggestion for young actors. Find monologues in this book that reflect your own personality, speaking style, and unique way of seeing the world. We're all wildly different. It should be no surprise, then, that the monologue you pick will be different from the one best suited for your friend – or the one your teacher assigns for you. Don't be afraid to stretch yourself, take some chances, and show an audience "the real you." Our individual quirks and eccentricities are what make us special. They also make us very interesting as actors.

There is an unfortunate reality of show business that needs to be addressed here too. A great deal of material written for children and teens, regrettably, has been abrasive, argumentative, and mean-spirited. Many scenes and monologues for young actors are drenched in sarcasm, cynicism, and snarkiness. I have always believed that young people deserve much better. There are many people in the acting profession, however, who think "drama" is synonymous with "conflict" or "argument." This is understandable, but is an overly simplistic and unnecessarily combative approach to actor training.

Ultimately, the confrontational approach does not take into account the vast range of human emotions necessary to perform truthful and realistic work in film, television, and theater. I'm also convinced that when young actors audition with angry monologues (berating a friend, classmate, or family member, for example) they make a big mistake. They establish a hostile, negative tone in the audition room. Young actors delivering monologues with negative, aggressive messages risk alienating industry professionals and audiences – the very same people we're all trying to entertain.

Nothing great was ever accomplished by a pessimist. U.S. President Calvin Coolidge said it best: "cynics do not create." Artists, however, do create. Our mission as performing artists is to create believable, sympathetic characters, draw audiences in, and hold people's interest and attention by telling compelling stories.

We create far more lasting value in this world when we surprise our audiences with inspiring, thought-provoking, and philosophical messages. When young actors offer deeper, stronger, more insightful messages than industry professionals normally hear in audition sessions, those performers will be fondly remembered long after those auditions are over.

Therefore, this book is intended to serve a dual purpose. It's meant to be two books in one. The primary goal is to give young actors audition material that is different enough to capture an audience's attention and stand out boldly from the crowd. Additionally, many of these monologues have an educational or inspirational focus. Consequently, if this book helps young actors voice positive, thought-provoking messages – and navigate safely past apathy, fear, uncertainty, and inertia – I'll consider that a valuable added benefit for actors, parents, teachers, and audiences alike.

I hope young actors will make the most of the material in this book. I hope you will make the most of every audition and training opportunity that comes your way. Above all, I hope you will make the most of yourself. I hope you will read this book until it is falling apart in your hands. I hope you will use these monologues to explore your interest in the performing arts, develop your skills, and reach your fullest potential as young actors. You can do it.

Mike Kimmel
Los Angeles, CA

A Brief Technical Note

A monologue of between one hundred fifty and one hundred sixty words in length roughly translates to one minute in performance time. Of the hundred monologues in this book, the first seventy-four fall into this category.

Some are a bit longer, running from one hundred seventy to one hundred eighty words. But they're still close enough to play nicely with the others.

If you're asked to perform a one-minute monologue, you should pick one from this first section. The remaining pieces are longer, ranging between two and three hundred words in length. These are intended for more advanced students — and for those times when you have the flexibility to perform a longer monologue (one to two minutes).

My best advice for young actors is to find a monologue that fits your personality well. Then work as hard as you can to make it your own. Pretend you're thinking these words up in your own mind — and speaking them out of your own mouth — when practicing and performing. Do your best to make the story realistic, conversational, and believable.

When you show the audience you believe the words you're speaking, your audience will believe those words and thoughts are your very own. Then the audience will believe you in that role you're performing. It's an incredible feeling when you realize your audience believes in you.

I believe in you too. Now go get 'em.

Lemonade for the Mailman

My Grandma Rose is absolutely ... amazing. One of the smartest ladies I ever met. Because she thinks of stuff other people don't.

Grandma saves food for the neighbor's dog. Leftover scraps of meat and chicken. She never throws away food. She didn't have a lot of food when she was growing up. So she doesn't like it if someone is hungry ... even someone's dog.

And every day at three o'clock, Grandma waits for the mailman. She noticed he was always running to finish delivering the mail. Not walking fast. Running. She asked why. He said they don't give him enough time ... and he has to hurry up to get to his second job. So Grandma started waiting for him every afternoon with a glass of lemonade.

How does someone even come up with that idea? I don't know. Nobody else waits for their mailman with a tall glass of ice-cold lemonade.

Except my beautiful Grandma Rose. None of her neighbors noticed. Everybody saw him running. Everybody thought he's ... just some worker guy who's always late. Maybe they even thought he's lazy.

But nobody else stopped to think ... maybe he's thirsty.

Big Screen TV

My parents bought a big screen TV. It's actually bigger than big. It's huge. Humungous.

Enormous. Gigantic. Pretty awesome. It's like going to the movies when we watch it. And we watch it all the time. Yep. All the time.

And that's kinda the problem. Lately, we ... watch it all the time. My whole entire family just wants to sit in the living room and watch movies.

Don't get me wrong. I like movies. Especially good movies. But sometimes I want to do something else. But nobody else wants to do something else. I'm the only else!

Nobody wants to go to the park. Nobody wants to go to the playground. Nobody wants to go to the mall. Nobody even wants to go for ice cream anymore. My family just wants to stay home and watch the big, giant movie screen TV all the time. All day long. All night long.

I don't know. I don't know about this new TV.

To tell you the truth ... I liked it better when we had our old TV.

Three Kinds of People

I don't know how my mother does it. Go, go, go ... all the time. Dad says she's an overachiever.

She's a principal in a school. Not my school, but that would be really cool if she was.

She also runs three miles a day. She ran marathons when she was younger ... but now she only goes three miles.

I think that's still a lot. So many people say they have no time to exercise. But Mom finds the time ... no matter how busy she gets. Dad says his wife can do anything.

Because she even wrote her first book. She was working on it for years. Finally got published last month. It's in the education field, and I think it's really gonna help a lot of people.

Mom says there are three kinds of people in the world. People who make things happen, people who watch what happens, and people who wonder what happened.

Guess which category my mom fits into. Correct!

Personally, though, I think she's in a category ... all by herself.

We'll Figure It Out

Do you know what's the hardest thing about being a kid? No? Grown-ups are always telling you what to do.

Yeah, yeah, I know. It's for our own good mostly. Safety stuff. Look both ways before crossing. Don't talk to strangers. Don't play with matches. Those things make sense.

But why do my parents' friends tell me what to study in college? Who to vote for when I get older? What kind of job to get? Those things are a million, billion years away.

And the kids I know are smart. We'll figure it out when we get there. So, come on! Have a little faith in us. Do us kids a favor. Don't talk down to us. Just because we're younger and littler than you doesn't mean we can't figure out stuff on our own.

Talk to kids like we're human beings. Listen to us too. And maybe ... adults can even learn something important from what kids are saying.

Kinda like ... you're doing right now.

The Waiting Room

I was in the doctor's office with my mother. We were sitting in the waiting room. Mom's fine. It was just a check-up.

Grown-ups do that every year. Kids too, I guess.

And I pulled out my phone. Like I always do when I'm waiting somewhere. Started playing a game. The new one I just got. Didn't really think about it. I just started playing on my phone.

It got real quiet in that waiting room. They didn't call anybody for a long time. So I looked up from my game and saw everyone else was on their phones too.

Except one person. My mom.

She was looking out the window and smiling. So peaceful. So calm. She looked ... gorgeous. I looked out that window too ... to see what she was looking at ... and smiling at.

There were two beautiful butterflies flying around in circles. Like they were dancing with each other. Amazing. And nobody except my mom even noticed. Nobody except my mom was watching. And smiling so sweet and so pretty.

Nutritious Snacks

My teacher said we all eat too much junk food. We have snack time. All the kids bring their snacks from home. But our teacher says most of us kids bring the wrong kind.

Cookies, candies, and cakes. The three "C's." All that sugary stuff. Those sugary sweets are no good for us. They just give people cavities and calories.

The kids get mad, but our teacher is right. We're supposed to eat healthy. Fruits and veggies. Nuts and seeds. Those are the healthy snacks your body needs. Those are nutritious snacks. They help us do better in sports and think better in school.

One of my classmates – who eats candy every day – says he'll change. He's going to start bringing nuts for snack time instead. Nuts instead of candy bars.

My teacher was so happy. She thought that was great. She asked ... what kind of nuts? Walnuts? Pistachio nuts? Macadamia nuts?

He said ... donuts.

The Clock Watching People

Did you ever notice how people watch the clock? Kids do that all the time. It's so rude. I call them The Clock Watching People. I pay attention to that stuff at school. It kinda bothers me when I see those same students start getting ... *fidgety* right before the bell rings.

And that's not right. They should be studying. Not looking at the clock. That shows they're not paying attention. They can't wait till class is over. They can't wait to run out when that bell rings.

Can I make a confession? I'm embarrassed when my class-mates act like that. Because we're in school to study. We're here to learn. Not sit around and watch the clock.

That's why I can't wait to get older. I can't wait till I'm all grown up. Because grown-ups are much more serious than kids. I bet grown-ups never, ever watch the clock at their jobs.

Isn't that right?

Right?

Uh ... right?

The Comfy Red Chair

Mom gave away my favorite chair today. It was sitting in our living room forever. Wasn't bothering anybody. Always did my homework there. So comfy. Dad used to fall asleep watching TV in it. It was his favorite chair too.

And when Dad was at work, our little doggie would sleep up there. Used to curl up in a ball and sleep there all day long. He could barely jump high enough to reach it. But he reached it.

Guess it was pretty comfy for Little Mister Hercules too. Especially with his arthritis. I didn't even know dogs could get that. Thought that was just a people disease. But our dog got it too. And a whole bunch of other bad stuff when he started getting old.

We put our little dog to sleep last month. Mama cried so much. We all got worried about her. Today she said she just couldn't stand looking at that chair without Little Mister Hercules sleeping in it anymore. My mother's very sensitive. That's why she got rid of everybody's favorite chair.

And now none of us have our favorite chair any more.

Or our favorite dog.

The Lady in the Booth

We just came back from vacation. A real long trip in the car. Six hour drive.

Some of that drive was a little boring. I started feeling grumpy. But we saw a lot of the country too.

On some of the roads, there were tolls. And there was one little spot out in the middle of nowhere with one little tollbooth.

In the little booth sat a little lady. Collecting the money and giving out change. Also gave us good directions. And was so nice and so friendly.

One friendly little lady out in the middle of nowhere. After we drove away, I started thinking about what she must be thinking about. Sitting in that booth all day long. Does she get bored? Like I got bored in the car?

If she does ... how does she stay so friendly and so happy whenever people drive up? Because it's a choice. Something someone chooses.

Some people get bored and choose grumpy.

Some people get bored and choose happy.

One Body Per Customer

My dad's getting a little heavy. He eats way too much. And he eats so fast sparks fly out of his knife and fork. That's definitely not healthy.

The doctor said she wants my dad to lose weight. Mom even bought him an exercise bike. Dad says he has no time to use it. Mom says we all have to take better care of the original equipment. We get one body per customer when we're born. No second chances.

If you use it right, one body is all you need. Lots of grown-ups take good care of themselves. They don't let themselves get heavy. They go jogging. They play tennis. Sometimes they go to the gym.

My dad could do that too. But he never listens to my mom. Never listens to the doctor. Never listens to anybody. He has a soundproof head.

But he's an awesome father. I think he's the nicest father in the whole, wide world. He takes such great care of me and my mom. And my brother and sister too.

I just wish ... he would take better care of himself.

Going for a Run

My dad took up running. He just wanted to lose some weight. He's getting better at it. Now he's training for a marathon. That's a twenty-six mile run! Twenty-six miles!

My mother says she gets tired if she drives twenty-six miles! I don't think Mom's gonna be running a marathon anytime soon. But that's okay. She plays tennis, and that's good exercise too.

But the funny thing is our neighbor. We've got a neighbor who never does anything. No exercise. None. Dad goes out for a real long run every Sunday. When Dad leaves, he sees this guy sitting on the couch watching the game.

Dad runs for three hours. Three hours! When he gets home, this guy is sitting in the same spot. He never moved! I don't know how somebody can sit still so long. Crazy, right?

So I'm glad my father is out there running instead. He's doing something good. Something positive.

I believe my father's gonna inspire a lot of people too. Starting with yours truly.

How Does He Do It?

My math teacher is the most awesome human being I ever met. He's a really good teacher. Knows all about math. Has tons of patience with us kids.

Always friendly. Plays nice with the other teachers. The Principal too. Yeah, I know. Teachers are supposed to be like that. To do all those things. And he does. But what's even more interesting is his outside life. Outside of school.

He's training for a triathlon. So he wakes up at four o'clock to start exercising. Running. Swimming. Riding his bike. All of the above.

He does all that before school starts. And when the first bell rings, he's full of energy. Never looks tired. Never slows down. Go, go, go all day.

And all day long he keeps a good attitude. Never complains about anything. He's even more inspiring than all the famous athletes on TV.

How does he do it? I don't know. I can't figure it out. But I'm really glad he figures it out.

I'm really glad he's my teacher too.

I Saw a Policeman

I was in the bank with my mother yesterday. I saw a policeman come in. I got a little nervous. I thought there was a problem in that bank. Maybe some bad guy was there.

So I watched that policeman very closely. But he didn't look worried. Totally calm. He got in line with all the other customers and waited. He just had to put in money like everybody else! Or take out money.

But the point is ... he's not like everybody else on that line. Everyone was looking at him. They weren't looking at the other customers. Only him.

I realized something. Being a policeman is not like a regular job. Because a policeman is always a policeman. Or a police-woman. If something bad happened in that bank, he would have to stop being a customer ... and start being a policeman again right away.

Nobody else has to do that. When other people finish work they're done. But not the police. That's why I think it's very hard to be a policeman. Or a policewoman. I think those police officers have a very hard job. One of the hardest jobs in the world.

New Old Sneakers

My dad just got another pair of new sneakers. Nice blue ones from the thrift store. They're barely used. But they're still used.

He got new ones at the regular store for me and my brother ... but he got his own from the secondhand thrift store. I guess they're a lot cheaper. And all clothing is half price on Sundays – so that's when he went. Late Sunday morning after he made us breakfast.

My dad buys all his own stuff at the thrift store. All our stuff at the regular store. He always puts us first. Dad says kids should have all new things ... because kids are completely new people.

Ever since Momma moved to Mr. Eddie's house ... my dad's been working at two different jobs. Grandma comes to watch us when he leaves for his night job. Because Dad's always running from his first job to his second.

That's why he needed more new sneakers. But I guess they're really his new old sneakers.

Red Socks

My father wears red socks. He works in a big office. Wears a suit and tie every day. But he has like a million, billion pairs of red socks too. Wears them all the time.

Me and my brother thought that was weird. A little embarrassing. Like Dad hangs out with Ronald McDonald or something!

But Dad says people shouldn't try to be like everybody else. Shouldn't put themselves in a little box. If everybody dresses the same, my dad likes to do something different. He doesn't care what other people think, either. He's says he's cool with it.

Dad says that's how he shows his personality.

So maybe ... that actually ... kinda makes sense. A lot of kids my age all try to be the same too. Act the same. Talk the same. Dress the same.

If everybody's exactly the same, it's like we're all part of one big puppet show or something. Not my dad. My father's nobody's puppet.

He's the man who's always wearing the red socks.

Sidewalks Are For Walking

Do you know what's the stupidest thing I ever saw? People riding their bikes on the sidewalk.

Yeah! The sidewalk!

That's not only stupid. It's dangerous and rude. I can't believe people actually do something like that. Especially when there's a separate bicycle lane in the street just for them! But they want to go riding fast on the sidewalk instead. Like race car drivers!

And that's completely against the rules. Because pedestrians *always* have the right of way. We learned that in school. And I worry about my grandmother walking around her neighborhood when people are doing dangerous things. And irresponsible things. So bikes have to ride in the street. With the cars, you know?

That's just logical. I'm not trying to be mean.

Cars drive in the street. So do motorcycles. And so should bikes! Everything with wheels. Everything wheely goes in the street ... not on the sidewalk.

Because sidewalks are for walking. That's why they're called side ... walks. And walking does not involve any kind of wheels.

The Almost Stop Sign

Did you ever watch drivers come to a stop sign? Most people never stop. They slow down. Roll through.

My Uncle Louie says stop signs are for people who don't know what they're doing. Beginning drivers. More experienced drivers – like him – can just slow down.

Uncle Lou explained that stop signs are more of a guideline than a rule. People who know what they're doing don't have to *really stop*. Just *almost stop*. Like a rolling stop.

But if it's rolling ... then it's moving! That's different than stopping! Uncle Lou's wrong. My father says we should always do the right thing. No matter what. Live your life like the whole world's watching.

I want to do things right. Even if the whole world's not watching. Just one person. Me. I'm watching myself.

When I'm old enough to drive, I'm gonna stop at every stop sign in the whole, wide world.

Because doing the right thing should never be our guideline. It should always be our rule.

17

Disgruntled

You know what I've noticed? There's a lot of people acting too grumpy. There's a word for it too. *Disgruntled*. That means unhappy and unsatisfied with the way things are.

Lotta disgruntled people out there these days. I'm telling you. I see it all the time. People are extremely disgruntled. Well, I don't like that attitude. I'm not a big fan of disgruntled. I'm here to get you gruntled. I want to see everybody get gruntled again.

I want to encourage people to get more gruntled. To get re-gruntled. I'd even like to gruntle up the whole world if I could.

Seriously, though. I think people get disgruntled because they're nervous. Everybody's stressed out. People are overwhelmed with work, school, family stuff. All kinds of obligations. That's why they all get disgruntled in the first place.

It's because they have so much going on that they feel overwhelmed. Never be overwhelmed. Instead, just be whelmed.

And always be gruntled.

Contains Peanuts

We were on an airplane. They gave us these little snacks. Itty bitty bags of peanuts. Pretty good, I guess. I read the bag to see what kind they were. It says in big letters ... *"Contains Peanuts!"*

Duh! Of course a bag of peanuts contains peanuts! A bag of peanuts better contain peanuts! That's the main ingredient! I get it though. They're worried some people are allergic. But come on! *"Contains peanuts"* on an actual bag of peanuts?! How stupid do they think we are?

Please don't answer that question.

Here's my opinion. I think you gotta let people figure out some things for themselves. The word *"Peanuts"* on the front should be enough. Because a bag of peanuts is always gonna contain peanuts. So if you can't have peanuts ... don't eat peanuts.

And here's some good advice. Free of charge. Don't eat peanut butter either. Peanut butter also contains peanuts.

An Ink Blot Test

You know what makes me mad? They made all us kids in school take a psychology test. A psychology test! They showed us these big, inky drawings. They call them the ink blot tests.

And then they asked what do we think it means! What does it mean? I know what it means. It means you should stop using these old fashioned fountain pens from Mr. Benjamin Franklin's office.

What's the matter with these people?! Using that old, antique fountain pen leaking ink ... and making ink blots everywhere. It's disgusting. Join the twenty-first century already.

Get a nice, modern little tablet. Get a stylus for typing on it. And boom! You're in business. What an idea!

They can take all the money they save on psychology tests and buy something good. Something better. Something to help them stop messing around with those messy ink blots.

And help them stop annoying kids with ink blot psychology tests. Now ... get some paper towels and help me clean up that ink! What a mess!

The Washing Machine Monster

My mom's not a big complainer. Not as much as most grown-ups, anyway.

But there's one thing that kinda bugs her around the house. Wanna know what it is? Socks.

Yeah, socks. She says our washing machine eats socks. Like an outer space monster! She washes a pair of socks and one of them disappears. Crazy, right?

She puts in two dirty socks. One clean one comes out. What happens to the other sock? Nobody knows. It disappears like a magic trick. And Mom gets really annoyed.

So I started thinking about this sock situation. I attacked it like an equation. Like a math problem in school. And I've created a solution. Wanna know what it is?

Here goes. The companies that make socks should make three, not two. Then we'll get three socks in a pair. One extra.

So the Washing Machine Monster eats a sock? Okay. We got an extra one in the drawer. A clean one. All ready to go. Problem solved. Washing Machine Monster defeated.

Boom. Done.

The Bad Cookies

They had cookies at school yesterday. I ate way too many. Again. I knew I shouldn't have. They weren't even good cookies, the kind I usually like. They were real cheap-o ones. Probably from the dollar store. That's what they tasted like, anyway. And stale too.

Nothing good could come out of that cookie box. So why did I even bother eating them? And eating them and eating them and eating them?

My mom says I have no "on-off switch." I guess she's right. Sometimes we gotta have self-control. Will power. That stops you from doing things you know you shouldn't do. And stops bad things from happening.

Because today I don't feel so good. If I had self-control yesterday, I'd feel better today. So that means I did this to myself. My fault. Gotta be more careful from now on.

I feel bad from this little mistake. I don't like feeling like this.

And I know that making worse mistakes makes us feel even worse. So ... no more bad cookies from now on. And no more bad decisions.

Only good cookies and good decisions.

The Opposite

I've got two kids in my class who are never prepared. They never do their homework. Never participate. Never study for a test.

I look at them and say – "*I don't want to be like that.*"

I'm not trying to be mean. Not trying to tell them how to act in class. Not at all. I just decided what they do ... is not for me. I wanna do better. So I asked myself how. Finally figured out if I want to be different, then I gotta do the opposite of everything these two kids do.

If I act differently, I'll get different results.

So now I do extra studying. Now I raise my hand twice as much. Now I do more homework.

And that's how I'm doing everything. That's what I'm doing from now on.

When I see something I don't think is right ... I figure out what would be the opposite ... and that's exactly what I start to do. The opposite!

Bigger and Better

My mother had a baby. It was me. I know because I was there. Actually, I don't remember a whole lot about it because I was very young at the time. Humble beginnings.

But that was my beginning. That's how I started out. From there, I got bigger, started learning all kinds of new things. I went to school. Learned to read and write. Ride a bike. Play basketball. Learned to play video games real good. Real well, I mean, because I learned grammar too.

Started getting better and better at everything. Started doing everything bigger and better. You can't do that all at once, but you can start learning. Start getting bigger and better. Before you know it, you're helping other people ... younger kids ... read and write. Ride their own bikes. Crush their own video games.

Step by step.

You can become a mentor, teacher, coach for younger kids. And help them grow bigger and better. It's an awesome thing to do. When you start getting bigger and better yourself.

That Fancy Coffee Place

My dad goes to that fancy, schmancy coffee place. You know, that big pretty one. Mom says it's too expensive so she always makes her own coffee at home.

Dad says you get what you pay for. The fancy, schmancy coffee place may be more expensive ... but when you taste the coffee they brew ... you'll see where your money goes.

And that's the funny thing about my parents. They don't agree on anything. They really don't. I don't know how they ever got together in the first place. How did they decide where to go on their first date?

Beats me.

Maybe it's true that opposites attract. Or maybe there's something else going on ... besides the coffee ... in my parents' marriage.

Because they get along together so well. They talk so sweet. They treat each other so nice. Better than any of my friends' parents.

And if they love each other that much ... well ... who the heck cares what kind of coffee they drink?

The Complaining Complainer

My mom says nobody ever solved a problem by complaining about it. Pretty good advice, huh?

I don't think I've ever heard my mom complain once. Not once in my whole, entire life.

Anytime something doesn't go exactly right for her, she doesn't complain. Instead she asks – *"How can I fix it?"*

I think that's smart. I know kids who complain about everything! They complain about school, homework, teachers ... even lunch!

My teacher complains too! She complains to the class about her grown-up stuff. She shouldn't do that. She's supposed to set a good example.

Mom's the one who sets the good example. She doesn't complain and she doesn't make excuses. Mom says if we all took the time we waste complaining ... and tried fixing stuff instead ... we wouldn't have anything left to complain about!

"If it's to be, it's up to me." That's my mom's favorite saying. From now on, it's my favorite saying too. Try it yourself. And maybe you won't have anything to complain about, either.

The Interrupting Interrupter

I've got one weird kid in my class. She always interrupts the teacher. I never saw anything like it in my whole entire life!

We call her the "Interrupting Interrupter from Interruption Junction."

She interrupts our teacher with a million questions. Every day! Doesn't even raise her hand. And the teacher lets her get away with it!

I don't think she's trying to be rude. But it is rude! It's rude to all the other students.

Because our teacher stops what he's doing. Then we never get back to where we were when we got interrupted. That's not fair to the rest of us.

I understand she has questions. But our class is not her own private tutoring session. It's our group class! And the rest of the group never complains. Never says anything. The silent majority. Well, I'm not being silent any more. Interrupting is just plain rude! And interrupting a big, giant group of people is rude times ten.

The Promise Keeper

My family went to the worst restaurant last night. Terrible food. Terrible service. Terrible everything. Dad says we went there three times. Mom asked him – *"Three times?"*

My father said – *"Yes. Last night was our first time, last time, and only time. We're never going back to that horrible, disgusting restaurant ever again."*

Dad's pretty funny. But very definite. When he says he's gonna do something ... he will. When he says he'll never do something ... he won't. When my father makes up his mind – that's it. Very strong decision maker. I can promise you that.

That's good. Because some people never make up their minds. And when they do ... they don't follow through. They're wishy-washy. They flip-flop. They never keep promises they make to anybody. Not even themselves.

My dad's a promise keeper. Learns from mistakes too. He picked that restaurant. So the next place he takes us to eat will be a whole lot better.

I can promise you that.

My Summer Vacation

Wanna hear about my summer vacation? No, I didn't think so. Nobody does. Except teachers. Every teacher I ever had in my whole entire life asks about my summer vacation. I always get that assignment at the beginning of every new school year! They always ask us to write an essay about our summer vacation.

I guess I understand why. That's like an introduction. How teachers meet the new kids in their class. The ones they never met before.

But kids get bored writing that same old, same old assignment every year. Some kids get so bored they even cheat! They recycle the same essay every year. They say it doesn't matter because the new teacher doesn't know it's the same essay they turned in the year before.

Is it cheating if you copy from yourself? I don't know. That's a tough one. I'll have to ask my dad. Because he has to write an expense report for his job every month. But he hands in the same report month after month after month. So I think my dad will probably say it's okay.

The Tick Tock Clock

My grandfather is the smartest man in the whole, wide world. He knows everything about cars, about the government, and about money too. And Grandpa always knows what time it is.

Grandpa wears a watch. He calls it an "old school tick tock clock." Grandpa says a gentleman should always wear a wristwatch so he can stay on schedule, never be late, and help other people be on time too.

I think that's very smart. He says people nowadays have a clock on their phones and their phones in their pockets! So they never know the right time.

People see Grandpa's watch and ask him the time all day long. He always tells them the time and he never gets mad. *"That's a gentleman's job,"* Grandpa says.

Old school style.

That's how I wanna be when I grow up. Friendly, smart, and helpful. Helping everybody. Telling the time. Just like Grandpa. With my old school tick tock clock. Smart, friendly, and always right on schedule.

You can set your watch by my Grandpa. And you can set your watch by me.

Ginger Ale is Good for You

Did you ever drink a nice, cold glass of ginger ale? That's a soda. Old-fashioned kind of soda.

The only place I ever saw it is in my grandmother's house. I don't even know where she buys it. Maybe some super secret store only grandmothers know about. They all go there together to shop.

Because grandmothers know all kinds of cool stuff. Things the rest of us normal, mortal human beings have no idea about. That comes from years and years and years of experience that grandmothers get from being grandmothers for a long, long time. And mothers before that.

Example.

Ginger ale is good for a tummy ache. Grandmas know this. If I'm visiting my grandmother and I have a stomach ache, she gives me a nice, cold glass of ginger ale. It works right away. Better than anything from the medicine cabinet, I'll tell you that right now.

And that's just one of the many things I learned at Grandma's house.

Class dismissed.

The King of Sneakers

You should see my Uncle Jonathan. He has more sneakers than I ever saw in my whole, entire life. He could open a sneaker store just with what he has in his closet. Except they'd all be the same exact size. And that's no good for people with bigger feet and smaller feet.

So it might not be such a terrific store. But he's definitely a terrific uncle. He plays all kinds of sports. Baseball, basketball, hockey, weightlifting. He's in great shape. I guess that's why he's got all those sneakers. Must be a hundred different pairs in his sneaker closet. Maybe even more. Every brand, every style, every color.

My Aunt Lisa calls him The Sneaker King. She says she married a fashionista! I love that word! Uncle Jon says he needs all those different sneakers for all his different sports. Aunt Lisa says he's just trying to look cool.

But maybe they're both right. What's wrong with being a great athlete ... and a great uncle ... and looking cool doing it?

I think every family should have a fashionista like my Uncle Jonathan. And a Mrs. Fashionista like my Aunt Lisa.

Training for the Olympics

You oughta meet my Uncle Richard. He loves sports. Loves to watch sports on TV. Plays a lot of sports too. But not as much as he did when he was younger.

Uncle Rich tells everyone he's an Olympic runner. He goes running every four years. Pretty funny, right?

He makes good jokes. And like a lot of guys his age, he says he's gotta get back in shape. Then he always asks – *"Is it possible to get back in shape if you've never actually been in shape?"*

He's actually in pretty good shape now. Just not Olympics shape. But that's the problem with people! Kids and grown-ups too. Everyone compares themselves to the best in the world.

That's good for competition. But we're not training for the Olympics. Just training to be better than we are now. We can't all compete in the Olympics, but we can all compete with our-selves. We can improve ourselves ... one little tiny bit at a time.

So just try to get a little better than you were yesterday. Focus on progress. Not perfection.

Moving Sale

We went to a moving sale. Dad calls it a yard sale. Mom calls it a tag sale ... because they put price tags on all the stuff they're selling. And you wouldn't believe all the stuff they were selling! Man!

The nice lady whose house it was says it's amazing how much junk we accumulate. I think she's right. There were piles and piles of stuff. Books, magazines, movies, clothes, dishes, furniture.

That lady's moving and didn't want to take it all. But I knew she hated to let it go. Especially her movies. I could tell by the look in her eyes.

She had all these movies. On VHS tape. You don't even see those tapes any more.

But nobody wanted to buy them.

Nobody even has the machine to play those tapes. That technology hardly exists any more. It was awesome when it was new ... back in the day. It was so weird to see all those old school tapes. Boxes and boxes of them. Because it makes me wonder what's awesome today ... that everyone loves ... and nobody's gonna care about later.

The Piano Movers

My parents bought a piano. They delivered it last week. I watched them do it. And I felt really sorry for the guys who had to carry that thing up the stairs. Pianos are so heavy!

Piano movers! What kind of person signs up for a job like that? Who would even apply? That's gotta be the hardest job in the whole, wide world. And one of those moving men was just a little skinny guy too. Way smaller than my dad. Smaller than my mom even.

Makes me think about what I want to be when I grow up. Anything except a piano mover. But I guess that's what happens when people don't prepare themselves for their most favorite kinds of jobs. They settle for any old job they can find. I don't know about carrying pianos up the stairs, though. Not worth the money, I think. No matter how much they pay me. Not even if they pay a million, billion, thousand dollars.

Piano moving is absolutely, positively the very last job on my personal wish list.

Is Anyone Perfect?

Do you know anyone who is perfect? No, me neither.

We all have our stuff to work on. That's normal. But I hear people say something strange. They won't try something new ... until they know they can do it perfect.

Isn't that weird? Because how can they do something perfect ... I mean perfectly ... adverb .... If they never even did it before?

That doesn't make any kind of sense. When you try something new ... you gotta be willing to mess it up. Do it all wrong. Make mistakes. That's part of learning.

It's like swimming. Or riding a bike. Or doing anything new. You gotta practice it a whole bunch of times. And maybe mess up a few of those practices. But you always learn from the mistakes. And do better next time.

But you gotta get started. You don't have to be great to start. But you have to start to be great. Practice doesn't make perfect. But it does make us better.

And better and better and better.

The Adult School

My Uncle Charlie goes to school at night. They call it an adult school. He's in the same exact classroom as high school kids are in during the day.

Except Uncle Charlie goes at night. There's a whole bunch of other grown-ups in his classroom too. That's why they call it an adult school. My uncle didn't do so good in school when he was young. But now he's forty years old and he's doing a million times better. Maybe a billion times better. He never finished high school when he was a teenager, but he's going to finish now.

My Uncle Charlie says you're never too old to learn. But to do something you've never done before you have to become a new kind of person. Someone you've never been before.

So I'm glad they have an adult school for people like Uncle Charlie. Because my uncle's getting a second chance. Everybody needs a second chance sometimes in life.

Everybody deserves a second chance too.

Three Vocabulary Words

My father had a good idea. To learn three new vocabulary words every day.

It sounds like a lot. But it really is not. He said just listen carefully all day long. And every time we hear a word we don't know – write it down.

Then we'll talk about it at night. Instead of watching TV. Dad will give us the definition. Then we can all think up ways to use that word in a sentence.

Personally, I think this is a very good idea. A lot of kids say "like" and "you know" too much. I want to speak better than that. I want to have a good vocabulary when I grow up. Even before I grow up.

So I listen for new words. Every day. When I hear people talk. When I watch TV. I'm always listening for the new words. And I'm writing down all the new words I hear. So write 'em down too, okay?

Write 'em down! Write 'em down! Write 'em down!

All right? Class dismissed.

Hydrate! Hydrate! Hydrate!

Ew vocabulary word. Write this down. Hydrate!

Do you know what that means? Don't worry. I didn't either. It's a big, fancy word for drinking water.

Because most people don't drink enough water. So they get "dehydrated." That's another vocabulary word, actually. Write that down too.

We learned in science that the Earth is 70 per cent water. And our bodies are 70 per cent water. So we have to drink tons of water. Just to maintain. To be in proper balance.

Or we won't feel so good. We'll feel sluggish and tired. But what do most people drink? Soda! That tastes good, but it's terrible for us.

When my mother was a teenager, she drank soda all the time. She drank it so much they called her the Soda Queen. But she changed. She got better habits. Smarter habits. Healthier habits.

Now she's always hydrating. Maybe I'll start calling her the Water Queen. Or maybe even Aqua-Woman. That would be a good nickname for my new, smart, healthy mom.

Agree to Disagree

You know what really stinks? Every time there's a big sports game – on TV – kids at school start arguing about which team is better.

Same with my parents. Every time there's an election –you know, in the government – Mom and Dad argue about which politician they like better.

It's like that book I read over the summer. *Gulliver's Travels.* People in the book argued about which side to crack open an egg. The fat side or the skinny side.

But that's the whole point. There's always two sides. Two sides to every story. Two sides to every game, every election ... even every egg.

Which one's better? How should I know? Maybe both sides have some good ideas. Maybe they're both half right. That's why I think people argue too much. Kids and grown-ups both! They never try to see the other side's point of view.

I wish they did. Maybe then people could finally learn ... to agree to disagree.

Sleeping Way Too Much

My older brother sleeps way too much. He says he never sleeps past eleven. Yeah, right. AM or PM?

Actually, my whole family is like that. We all sleep too much. Me too. I need to sleep ten hours. But sometimes ... eleven feels so good, I wanna try for fourteen.

But I can't get away with that on a school night. None of us can. That's why I love holidays. Did you ever notice that all the really good holidays give you a day off from school? And isn't it funny how the most famous people were always born on holidays? Weird, right?

Especially Abraham Lincoln. His birthday is my favorite holiday. Because he was the best President ever. Got a feeling he only slept a normal amount. That's probably why he accomplished so much with his life. Why he was so inspirational.

So I always celebrate his presidency, his life, and his work. Every year on Lincoln's birthday ... I send a nice birthday card to Daniel Day Lewis.

The Greatest

My Uncle Mike – the teacher – met Muhammad Ali – the boxer. The boxer they called "The Greatest." He was champion like a million times.

My uncle met him years ago. They even sparred together. Not in a boxing place, but in a magic place. A magic store that magicians go to.

Because Muhammad Ali used to do magic tricks. He became a really good magician ... because he had such fast hands. Those fast hands worked just as well for magic as they did for boxing.

That goes to show you. A person can have different interests. A person can be more than just one thing. A person can study and be good at two different things. Or even more!

Like Muhammad Ali was great at boxing and also magic. Like my uncle is great at magic and also teaching.

And that means us kids can be great in school ... and also great at something else. And the something else can be anything we choose.

Because we can choose to be anything we want to be in life.

Even ... The Greatest.

The Best of the Best

How does someone get to be the best? In any kind of thing they do. School, sports, music. Anything.

Example. Who's the best basketball player ever? Michael Jordan.

Yeah, yeah, I know. Some people say it's that other guy. But I say Michael Jordan was the best ever.

Guess how he got there. Hard work and practice. Practiced all the time. Didn't start out so good. Got cut from his high school team. Wasn't even as good as those other teenagers. He went home and cried that day.

But the next day ... he started bringing his own basketball to school. He went an hour early to practice by himself before school even opened. Day in. Day out. Did that for a year.

And he improved a whole lot. Enough to make his high school team. Enough to play in college and the pros. Enough to be the greatest player ever. Best of the best.

Enough for the whole world to still keep talking about him now ... even so many years after he retired from playing professional basketball.

Chocolate, Chocolate, and More Chocolate

I'm learning to cook. Not really cook, but bake. Because desserts are my most favorite thing in the whole wide world. I like every dessert they ever invented.

Especially anything with chocolate. My mom was gonna make her famous banana nut muffins. I talked her into making chocolate chip muffins instead. Much better choice.

And since we were using chocolate chips, I added cocoa to the batter. So we made chocolate chocolate chip muffins.

And when they were done, they were piping hot. Yum! Since they're hot, wouldn't it be great to melt some chocolate over the tops? I'm glad you asked that question! Yes, it would! So yes, we did!

Melted some bakers' chocolate over the hot muffins. Let them cool. Then popped them in the freezer for an hour. Yes, indeed. They were an instant hit. And that's how I invented chocolate covered chocolate with chocolate chips.

I'm very proud of this invention. And I believe ... the Nobel Prize Committee is going to be very impressed. Very interested in this exciting new discovery of mine. Yum!

Assassinating Pumpkins

I'm boycotting Halloween. Worst holiday they ever invented, if you ask me.

Not just because of all the ghosts and goblins and witches. But also because of the jack-o-lanterns.

They assassinate all these perfectly healthy, lovable pumpkins to make those stupid, horrible jack-o-lanterns. They carve them up with a carving knife. Probably the same big, giant knife The Farmer's Wife used on the Three Blind Mice. Who couldn't defend themselves either, by the way.

Every Halloween, they carve pumpkins up like nobody's business. Spill their guts and seeds out all over the table. We could have used those seeds to grow new baby pumpkins to feed people! Who knows how many pumpkin pies never got baked because the people wanted to use those pumpkins to scare little kids with instead.

You never see anybody carving up honeydews, cantaloupes, or even watermelons to make decorations for any other holidays! So why do they have to pick on my poor defenseless pumpkins every October? Who decided that was okay? Where is that written?

There outta be a law ...

The Legend of Jan-Tastic

Did you meet my Aunt Kim? When she was in high school, she was friends with this girl Jan. Still great friends.

Everybody called her Jan-Tastic. Cool nickname, right? Like a superhero name. That describes Jan perfectly.

When anyone needed help studying, guess who they went to? Correct! Jan-Tastic was a straight A student. Especially math and science.

She's still great with math and science. Works as a dietitian in a big hospital. Helps people eat healthy, get healthy, and stay healthy.

Few years ago, Jan-Tastic learned an old classmate – John – was in real bad shape. Needed a new kidney to stay alive. Jan-Tastic didn't think twice. She volunteered. She donated her kidney to save his life. Now he gets to live longer!

Today ... Jan and John are both doing fine. Healthy and strong.

People can be so selfish sometimes. Right? So imagine someone giving her kidney to a classmate she hadn't seen in fifteen years. Strong! Brave! Amazing! Unbelievable!

What a totally Jan-Tastic thing to do!

Our Friends in Australia

There's a new kid in my class from Australia. Australia! Really nice kid too. Good manners.

But the other kids have been a little rude to him. Not on purpose ... I don't think. But they all come up to him and say the same things. They ask the same goofy questions all the time.

— *"Do you see kangaroos every day?"*

— *"Do they jump over your fence?"*

— *"Do koala bears come in your house? Can they fit through a doggie door?"*

— *"Can you teach me how to throw a boomerang?"*

You know, if you act this way to our friends in Australia ... they're not gonna be our friends very long. So how do you treat an Australian? Easy! Treat an Australian like you'd treat anyone else!

Just because he's from Australia doesn't make him an expert on kangaroos, koala bears, and boomerangs. He's a kid just like us. Except he's from the other side of the world.

And ... well ... maybe he's got better manners too. No ... definitely. He's definitely got better manners. And you don't get good manners from throwing boomerangs ... I'll tell you that right now.

The Beginning

You know what I think? I think it's hard to be a kid,

When we're kids, everything is brand new. Because we're so young! If we want to try something ... if we want to learn something ... we're always doing it for the first time. So we always have to figure out how to start.

Always at the beginning.

When we learned to read, we started at the beginning. Riding bikes? Had to keep falling down. Starting at the beginning.

Someday, when we get jobs, we'll start at the beginning too.

The good news is ... everybody started at the beginning. So we can do what they did. Even copy them. This is one time it's okay to copy.

Because things are hardest in the beginning. Then they get easier. No mystery any more. In the middle, we're already in motion. In the end, we look back and realize it wasn't as hard as we thought.

So get started! Move! Baby steps are okay. Sometimes that's the best way to do it ... in the beginning.

Nobody Says "Thank You"

Wanna hear something weird? Good. I'm telling you anyway. People have forgotten how to say "*Thank you.*" Nobody says "*Thank you*" any more. I never really noticed, but Aunt Adele pointed it out to me.

She says things were different twenty, thirty years ago. The average person was much more polite. But now people have zero social skills. No manners at all. They run around doing whatever they want, acting like a bunch of pirates or something.

They don't say, "*Please.*" They don't say, "*Thank you.*" And they definitely don't say, "*You're welcome.*" That's probably impossible for them. They couldn't do it if they tried. Those two words are not even in their vocabulary. It's like asking a cat to bark.

We have a less polite society. That's it. In my opinion, that's what's wrong with our whole, entire planet. That's the world according to me. And don't bother thanking me for this explanation, either.

I honestly don't think I could stand it.

You Don't Know Jack

There was a great story about Jack Nicholson. My mother's favorite actor. Been in a million movies.

He was in this acting class when he was young. When he was just getting started, before he got famous. He performed a scene with a partner. Then they both sat down in chairs on stage to hear from the teacher. That's how they do it in Hollywood.

This teacher didn't like what Jack Nicholson did. Didn't think he was acting too well.

Told Jack all the things he did wrong – in front of the whole class. Pretty embarrassing, right?

Then the acting teacher finishes up, saying – *"It's just not there, Jack."*

Mr. Nicholson listened, stayed calm, and answered – *"Maybe it's there and you can't see it."*

I love that! He was so confident! He believed in himself when his teacher didn't. And he became one of the biggest movie stars.

So ... he was right to believe in himself.

Sometimes we have to believe in ourselves when nobody else does. Especially when nobody else does. Because the experts aren't always right. Sometimes ... they don't know Jack.

Small Potatoes

We were watching this reality show on TV. The one with all the business people. People inventing stuff. People starting up big companies. And everybody was laughing at this one guy. It made me really mad too ... because he was trying so hard.

Nobody liked his business idea. They said he was thinking too small. Way too small. They said he was small potatoes.

But sometimes you have to start small. Start small and just put one foot in front of the other. That's progress. Little by little. That's how Bill Gates started. Mark Zuckerberg too. Even Jeff Bezos. They all started small. They worked hard. Then they blew up. They became huge.

So never count someone out just because you think they're not doing something big enough.

Don't make fun of small potatoes. Because ... you never know. Small potatoes are where tater tots come from. Tater tots are a lot of people's favorite. They're my favorite too.

You know how many tater tots they sell in stores, malls, and restaurants every day? Lots! Lots of tots! That's definitely not small potatoes.

Perfume and Cologne

Why do grown-ups wear so much of that stuff? Perfume and cologne, I mean. Men and women both.

No, I get it. They wear it to smell good. Of course. But why do they put on so much of it – instead of just a normal human being amount?

They don't need that much. Right? My mom and dad spray it on, but just a tiny little bit. That's all you really need. That's enough to make most ladies and men smell pretty good.

But some people spritz on ten gallons of that stuff. Wow! It smells so strong, I have to hold my nose when they walk by.

Makes me wonder how bad they think they smell without it. Maybe they think they're really stinky. So stinky people will hold their noses when they go by.

But if people cover their noses because of the strong fragrance ... then it's the same result anyway! So stop wasting your money on all that perfume and cologne, people. You smell fine. Just use your natural, original, human being smell.

Goody Two Shoes

I tell my friends – "*Do your homework.*"

I tell my friends – "*Don't litter.*"

I tell my friends – "*Clean up after yourself in the cafeteria.*"

My friends say I turned into a goody two shoes. Well, I wish I could go further. I'd like to do better. I'd like to be a goody three shoes! Because a lot of kids aren't even a goody one shoe!

Too many kids don't act good at all. Adults too. So if I act a little gooder – I mean better – maybe I'll make up for some people who don't try hard enough. Or act good enough.

Because we can all do better. My dad says the biggest room in the world is the room for improvement. Funny, right? Also true.

You know what the smallest room in the world is? A mushroom! That's just a joke. See? We can act nice, be a goody two shoes ... and still have fun.

Right? Of course right!

The Race Car King of California

Isaw the most awesome show on television. A story about this race car driver guy. He's also a Hollywood stuntman. He does racing car stunts on all kinds of movies.

Sammy Maloof. And there were like a million times the cars and trucks he drove got all smashed up. But he was still okay inside. Not even a little scratch. Amazing. It's like he's protected or something.

And when he's not racing cars and making movies ... he goes all over the world doing outreach work for kids. He gives little kids rides in his stunt car. The kids love it.

They call him the Race Car King of California. And now his daughter races cars too! Hannah Maloof! She's Sammy and Jennifer's daughter. She's only twenty-one years old! Not much older than my big sister. And she's amazing too. Drives great ... just like her dad!

Maybe driving great runs in the family. And maybe we'll start calling Hannah ... the Race Car Princess of California! Hey! Kinda got a nice ring to it ...

Vrooom! Vrooom! Vroooom!

The Talented Twins

There are these two girls ... Meghan and Kaitlyn. Nineteen years old. They're twins. The prettiest twins you ever saw in your whole entire life.

They're actors too. But ... they don't act like most pretty girls in acting act!

Let me explain. They draw. They ride skateboards. They do all kinds of sports. They practice martial arts. They learned boxing. They work on cars too. They know how to drive cars. They even know how to fix cars. Wild!

I never saw two teenage girls who know how to do all the things they know how to do!

I guess because their parents are the same way. They do a million different things too. So they started teaching their twin daughters how to do a million different things – ever since they were little.

And that's the secret. A person doesn't have to be just one thing. A person can learn all kinds of stuff and grow up to be a million different things.

And there's two of them ... so they can be two million different things!

Baby Dinosaurs

Two words. Baby dinosaurs. Give me your honest opinion.

Would you consider them cute because they're babies? Or ... are they just miniature versions of the big, giant scary monsters they're gonna grow into someday?

What do you think?

They're babies, and all babies are cute, right? Even if they have green scales and pointy tails.

To their mommy and daddy dinosaurs, they're still cute and adorable. But when they grow up to look like their mommies and daddies, they're gonna be pretty frightening. Like the grown-up dinosaurs in those movies.

So – are baby dinosaurs cute or scary? Both opinions are equally valid. Okay. I know I've given you a lot to think about. So take your time. Digest it all. Take some notes. Write down your thoughts and make a decision on this topic.

Baby dinosaurs. Cute or scary?

I'll expect a full report on my desk Monday morning.

Class dismissed.

Mr. Rhinoceros Man

We went to the zoo last week. Out of all the animals, I couldn't stop looking at the rhinoceros. Weird looking animal, you know? My dad says a rhinoceros looks like a unicorn wearing armor ... like he's going into battle or something. Pretty funny, huh? Dad's got a good sense of humor. Sometimes.

But maybe we shouldn't make jokes about a rhinoceros. Probably wouldn't be too funny if he got loose, right?

And I wonder what Mr. Rhinoceros Man says about us? What does a rhino think about ... how we look? What do we look like to him, I wonder? A big piece of pumpkin pie? Maybe a moving target for him to zero in on with that scary looking horn?

We might look pretty weird to a rhinoceros because we're bopping around on two legs instead of four. The rhino doesn't know we're more than flesh and blood. We have thoughts, emotions, ideas.

And maybe vice versa. Maybe the rhino is more than just horns and armor too. Maybe he has thoughts, emotions, and ideas too.

Boy, I sure hope so ... because that's one very weird looking animal.

Weddings and Marriage and Stuff

You know ... I'm thinking about getting married.

No! Not now! Can't! I'm a kid! But I keep thinking about how people do it. How does someone know who to marry?

My dad married my mom. My grandfather married my grandmother. My uncle married my aunt. So why do I have to marry a stranger? Why am I the one who has to re-invent the wheel? Completely unfair.

And some people never get married. Like my Uncle Frankie. He's single. He was in love with this lady. Head over heels. Crazy about her. Wrote her a love letter every day for two years. Finally, she married the mailman.

And he's not alone. I mean ... he's alone because he's not married ... but he's not the only one. Lots of people never get married. They stay single.

But I think it's easier for ladies to be single than men. I do. It's more important for men to get married. My teacher explained it. He's been married forever. He says a man is not complete until he is married. Then he is finished.

Cheeseburger of the Year

My Aunt Dana and Uncle Tom are foodies. Did you ever hear that expression? I didn't even know that was a thing. But Dana and Tom say foodies are people who are real interested in ... food obviously! Cooking ... recipes ... restaurants ... everything about food!

They went to some kind of awards show too. They have all these different kinds of awards now for all these different kinds of foods.

The Best. The Newest. The Most Original.

They even give an award for best cheeseburger. Best cheeseburger! Cheeseburger of the Year Award! Who comes up with this stuff?!

No. Don't tell me. I don't think I want to know. Just let me know when they have a Milkshake of the Year Award. Maybe a Chocolate Chip Cookie of the Year Award. Those would get my attention.

And let me know if they need any judges, okay? I can be a foodie for those two contests anytime.

Anytime. Day or night. Rain or shine. Anytime. In fact ... just to show you how dedicated I am ... I'll start practicing right now.

Pay Attention to Stuff

Know what?

Some kids never pay attention. Like this boy in school. He's always distracted, doing something else. Never participates. Never helps our teacher. Never listens when you talk to him. His mind is always wandering. No focus at all. Not even a little teeny-weeny bit of mini-focus.

That's why he misses stuff. He forgets when we have a test. He never remembers his homework. He didn't know he was twelve until he turned thirteen!

But you can't act that way. It's not good. You gotta be on top of your game. You gotta pay attention to stuff. If not ... it's like you're running around all hypnotized. Half awake. Like that guy on TV who got hit on the head with a coconut and got amnesia.

That's no way to live. We're supposed to be alert. Wide awake. Otherwise ... we'll miss stuff.

So pay attention. Some of the things you're missing might be things you'd like if you didn't miss them. Might even be some of your brand new favorites.

I hope you'll take this advice. Uh ... are you listening?

Are you listening?

Awards Show and Tell

Me and my parents were watching the awards show on TV last night. Did you see it?

It was so long! Way long! Mom and Dad finally got disgusted. And they turned it off halfway through. Those announcers were just talking and talking. We want to see the actors. We want to see the singers!

Nobody wants to see the announcers yapping all night and making all kinds of goofy jokes when they give out the trophies.

And they should know this! They should know what people want to see. They're in the entertainment industry too. They're supposed to be the professionals. They're supposed to know what they're doing. But they don't realize they're talking too much!

The audience wants to see the people *getting the awards – not giving the awards*!

So beginning today, I'm gonna start noticing. I'm gonna start to notice when I'm talking too much. When I'm yapping on and on and on! When people start to tune me out ...

Oh no! Maybe I'm doing it now! Am I? Am I talking too much?

Uh ... uh ... goodbye!

The Astronauts

When I was little, I wanted to be an astronaut. Did you ever wonder what that was like? I wonder about that kinda stuff all the time.

Imagine being in the rocket ship on that long trip all through space. What do astronauts talk about with the rest of the astronauts up there? What do they think about in the middle of space?

What's it like to float around in zero gravity? What's it like to be so far away from home? So far that nobody can even come to your rescue if something goes wrong?

Just imagine standing on the moon ... and looking back at the Earth. How wild would that be?

Talk about having a unique perspective! That's what my grandpa says we should try to develop. So think about standing on the moon and looking back at the Earth.

Now that's what they call ... a whole new way ... a brand new way ... of looking at the world.

The Speech Therapist

My Aunt Rebekah is the coolest lady in the whole, wide world. One of the smartest ladies I ever met.

She's a speech therapist. Don't worry. I didn't know what that was either.

She specializes in kids. She works in a school. Aunt Rebekah helps kids who have trouble talking. And kids with hearing problems too. She went to school to study this for a long time. In college ... and even after college.

And when she was having her own baby ... my cousin Jordan ... she talked to him! I mean even before he was born. She used to talk to him when he was still in her tummy.

That's why my cousin Jordan is so smart. My Aunt Rebekah used to talk to him when he was in her tummy! How many ladies would even think of doing that when they're having their babies? Not too many, probably.

But then again ... not too many ladies are speech therapists.

Loud Talkers

Phones! Phones! Phones! Everywhere I go ... phones!

People on their phones everywhere! And sometimes it sounds like they're the only ones talking!

I wanna ask 'em – "*Hey! Is there someone on the other end of that line? Does the other person in your conversation have anything to say? Anything to contribute? Or just you?*"

Why are you talking non-stop into your phone like that? And so loud! Sometimes they talk to their phones so loud ... I can't even hear someone I'm talking to in person! Someone standing right next to me!

Quiet down, already! I like loud movies. I like loud video games. But you people are giving me a headache with all your loud talking.

My grandmother always says we have two ears and one mouth. So we should listen twice as much as we talk. That means talk half as much, people!

And please turn down the volume when you talk. Not just for my sake. You don't want to wake the baby.

Okay ... we don't really have a baby. But you're still talking way too loud.

Extremely Annoying People

Do you know any annoying people? I sure do. There's quite a few at my school.

Quite. A. Few.

Some of them click their pens. Some of them are tappers. They tap, tap, tap their desks all day, day, day long. Some of them pop their bubble gum. Pop, pop, poppity-pop, pop, pop. Then another pop.

A lot of my friends get very aggravated in school. They say it's so distracting they can't concentrate on what the teacher's saying. When other people act like that, they're being very inconsiderate. Right? Of course right!

But it doesn't really matter what *others do*, does it? What's much more important is *what we do*. It's a million times more important.

Because we can't control the whole entire world. Guess what we can control? Correct! Ourselves!

So take control of your own mind. Make your mind so strong it won't matter what anyone else says or does.

Because you're the only person who can think in your mind. So only think good thoughts. Today and every day. That's an order.

The Mighty, Mighty Cigarette

Cigarettes must be amazing. I don't smoke. I'm too young. I don't want to when I get older, either. They're much too smelly and smoky and stinky.

But I can't believe how much grown-ups love them. Cigarettes must be amazing.

Seems like grown-ups will do anything for a cigarette. We were in Minneapolis last year for Christmas. That's in Minnesota. It was freezing! I was never so cold in my whole, entire life! But this lady who worked at the hotel kept going outside to smoke. She didn't care how cold it was. She had to take a cigarette break out in the freezing cold. Cigarettes must be amazing!

Later, we were driving back to the airport. The neighborhood was kinda run-down and there were a lot of homeless people. They were asking for money ... and food. I felt so bad for them.

But some of them were smoking. So I thought – *"Wow! Some people buy cigarettes instead of food ... even when they're hungry! People like cigarettes better than food ... or keeping warm! Cigarettes must really be amazing!"*

I just don't get it. I still think they're much too smelly and smoky and stinky.

The Dangers of Stress

Can you believe my friend's father had a heart attack? He's thirty-eight years old. That sounds old to us kids, but grown-ups say thirty-eight is young for a heart attack.

He's better now, but they told him to make some changes. Doctor says he has to change his diet, stop smoking, do more exercise, and find time to play.

Play! Telling an adult to play! But lots of kids my age don't play enough, either!

And I don't mean video games. I mean going to the playground, running, jumping rope, playing basketball. Stuff like that. That's why so many kids get heavy. And there's no reason for it!

So I tell all my friends to go to the playground. And bring your mom and dad. Maybe invite your parents to go hiking or biking. Because grown-ups forget. Look what happened to my friend's father!

Sure, kids need grown-ups. But grown-ups need kids too ... to teach them how to play. They really do. Unfortunately ... my friend's father is proof.

So play today. Have fun. Relax. Be happy. And be healthy too. Go play. That's an order.

Arts and Crafts

We had an arts and crafts project in school today. I never really liked that stuff ... until now. Our teacher put all the projects from our class together at the back of the room.

And ... I don't know. It's different when you see them all together.

Isn't it amazing how they can make all kinds of cool things out of nothing? Stuff people just throw away. Bottle caps, toothpicks, popsicle sticks. Cardboard, old newspaper, pipe cleaners, string, buttons. All that weird stuff nobody knows what to do with ... except Arts and Crafts people.

Reminds me of that old TV show my parents watch, *Gilligan's Island*. One time the Professor made a lie detector out of coconuts. Sounds impossible, but I guess the Professor was just that smart.

My parents call that creative thinking. Thinking outside the box. Exactly the kind of thinking they use to come up with all those Arts and Crafts projects.

Pretty smart.

So put on your thinking cap. You never know. You might think up something pretty smart too. With or without coconuts.

Do You Have Any Questions?

Wanna hear something weird? No? Good, I'm telling you anyway.

My teacher always asks – "*Do you have any questions?*"

Every day. Every lesson. She always asks. Because she's a *great* teacher. But ... how do I say this nicely? Uh ... okay ... some of the kids in my class are *not* great students!

Don't get me wrong. They *can* be great students ... but they have to try harder! Much harder! Most of them never even try a little.

They never participate in class. They never raise their hands. They never ask a question.

Then – later – they say they didn't understand what we did. That's crazy, right? Because our teacher asked! "*Do you have any questions?*"

And if you don't understand something ... you have to raise your hand! That's the way it works ... for kids and for grown-ups too. All over the planet. Ask a question. Get an answer.

That's a pretty simple rule. The rule for school.

Got it? Understand? Do you have any questions?

I repeat – "*DO YOU HAVE ANY QUESTIONS?*"

The Power of Shoelaces

I stayed at Grandma's last weekend.

They were painting our apartment ... and my mom thought I would be more comfortable with *her mom*. That way I wouldn't have to smell the paint fumes.

Good idea because I don't like the way paint stinks. Probably nobody likes it ... but especially me.

Anyway ... I was going outside to play basketball ... and was trying to hurry up. And I pulled too tight on my shoelace and it broke. I don't like when that happens. Probably nobody likes when that happens ... but especially me.

Those were my only sneakers. I don't have another pair. So I figured that was it. No basketball ... unless I wore my regular shoes.

Then Grandma went in the kitchen drawer and pulled out ... shoelaces. Short shoelaces, long shoelaces, white shoelaces, black shoelaces. Even striped shoelaces and red shoelaces!

Grandma always has extra stuff people need. Grandma always knows what to do. She's amazing. Unbelievable.

I really appreciate her. Probably everybody appreciates their grandmother ... but especially me.

Hurry Up. Take Your Time.

Mom always tells me to hurry up.

Grandma always says – "*Slow down. Take your time.*"

Two different kinds of advice. Complete opposites. Both are intended for our good.

But ... I can't do both ... right? When I hurry up, I make mistakes. I think we all do.

When we hurry up, we get mixed up. We can make ourselves confused. Too much nervous energy. Makes us bounce from thing to thing. Like a gumball bopping around inside a soda can.

It's moving all over the place, but it's not getting anywhere.

So ... yes, we have to move forward, but not with all that nervous energy bouncing around all over the place.

You gotta be calm to get where you wanna go. Our ships come in over a calm sea. So I say ... if someone tells you to hurry up, then you tell them to wait.

Because you're the only person who can think in your mind. And to think takes time. So never hurry. Take your time. And always take time to think.

Do you agree ... or disagree? What do you think? Let me know. Take your time too. Take all the time you need.

Help With The Chores

My mom said I had to start helping with the chores.

Chores?! Chores?!

What?! Are we living on a farm or something? We live in a one-bedroom apartment on the seventeenth floor of this big, giant building!

What kind of chores? Feeding the chickens? Milking the cows? Quacking the ducks?

What year is this anyway?! Because maybe my mom thinks we're living in the old West?! Way back in the cowboy days?

Back then, everybody had chores to do. If you wanted a fire, you had to rub two sticks together until you got a spark. If you wanted eggs for breakfast, you had to make sure your chickens were doing their chores! And keep them safe from coyotes and other wild animals too.

And if you wanted meat, well ... you had to find some kinda meat that runs slower than you run!

So if Mom wants me to help at home ... I can help at home. I'll help with laundry, cleaning, cooking ... anything. But those aren't chores. Back in the old time days ... the cowboy days ... THOSE were chores!

Grandma's Famous Banana Bread

My grandmother makes the best banana bread in the whole wide world. Makes it from scratch. Doesn't even use a recipe.

Everybody who tastes it says it's the best. It's so delicious I wish I was twins. Then I could eat twice as much. That's crazy, right? But that's how good it is!

Grandma Sharon says it's no big deal. *"That's what grandmothers do,"* she tells me. *"We take care of people. We feed people. We feed everyone in the world with all the yummy things we cook ... and bake."*

I think that's why grandmothers were invented. Why they came to this planet in the first place. That's their job.

But even if every grandmother feeds people, I still think my Grandma Sharon does it better than all the other grandmothers combined. And I still wish I was twins so I could eat twice as much of her yummy banana bread. But ... maybe triplets or quadruplets would be even better.

You definitely have to try some of her banana bread when you come visit. Because it's better than good. It's the best in the West! And East and South and North!

New Kid in a New School

I remember being the new kid in school. It was pretty scary at the time. I didn't know what to expect.

Didn't know where my classroom was going to be. Didn't know any of the other kids. Didn't know if my teacher was mean or nice. Didn't even know where the bathrooms were.

To tell you the truth, I was afraid of walking into that building the first time. It was so new, so big, so different from my old school.

But now it feels so familiar, so comfortable, so much like home.

Just goes to show you. Most of the things kids worry about ... aren't worth worrying about. Because they're not even real.

And a lot of things are only scary in the beginning.

But ... now ... it's much different. Honestly ... I couldn't imagine being in a nicer school.

I don't think there is a nicer school. But if there is ... and I had to go there today ... I wouldn't be worried or nervous at all.

Not even one, teensy, tiny little bit.

Longer Scenes
for
Advanced Students

The Greatest Gift

What is the greatest gift you've ever received?

Was it a toy? Maybe a new bicycle? Or even a book? That's a really good gift too, you know. Well ... it is for some kids.

But think about this. Did you ever have a new little brother or sister join your family? That's what we call ... the gift of life.

Nowadays, our world is very different. Things are not like they were years ago. Some of us kids don't even live with our natural-born mothers and fathers. We have all different kinds of families now. With half-brothers and sisters, step-brothers and sisters, and foster brothers and sisters. All very different. And that's okay.

Because the greatest gift is still the same. The greatest gift to receive is a new baby ... a new little addition to our families. And the greatest gift we can give back is the same one too. It's just reversed. The greatest gift to give is to be a terrific big brother or big sister for that new little addition to your family.

Always remember this. No matter what else changes in this world, my friends ... those are still the two greatest gifts of all time.

The Butterfly Effect

Did you ever think about the effect you – yes, I mean you – have on the rest of this planet? That's okay. I didn't either.

They say even the flapping of a butterfly's wings can be enough to change the weather. They call that the butterfly effect.

But we all have an effect. We make some kind of impact with everything we do.

Almost like what they call your carbon footprint ... but bigger. Like a carbon head print. Maybe a full body print.

Like making a snow angel with your body in space and time. Flapping your own butterfly wings. And that changes everything. Everything in this world ... and maybe everything in all the other worlds out there too.

Let me explain. Everything we do affects everything else. So anything you change could have a big effect. Like setting off a string of dominoes. And then bigger dominoes. And then even bigger. Times infinity.

So we've got a ginormous responsibility! Not to mess things up for all the other kids on the planet. And their kids ... and their kids' kids. Over and over and over again. Times infinity.

Do you understand? Good. I'm glad we had this little talk today. Aren't you? I hope it has an effect on you ... a butterfly effect.

The Talent Agent

My dad says nowadays ... everybody is a specialist. Everyone has their specialty.

Even with acting. Some people specialize in comedy. Other people prefer drama. And some even specialize in acting for commercials.

And there are teachers who specialize in teaching kids acting. That helps kids who don't even want to act. Kids who are shy and just need more confidence talking in front of people.

I have an agent now who specializes in kids. They're awesome too! All their actors are young kids and teenagers. They found auditions and parts for so many people! And I'm one of them! It's great because I wanted to act ever since I was little. And now I'm finally doing it.

I love what I'm doing too. But I couldn't do any of it without my awesome talent agent. And everybody in the office. They talk to people and find the auditions. Then I have to do MY job. Study, prepare, show up, and nail it!

And when you really knock it out of the park at an audition, you have a good shot at booking that job. But nobody would ever book any job without a talent agent to find those auditions in the first place.

Because a good talent agent connects the dots ... between actors who want to act ... and producers who need actors for their shows. And nobody can do anything in show business ... without that one smart person ... behind the scenes.

A good talent agent who knows how to connect all the dots for all their people.

And Then There Was One ...

My older sister was in a martial arts tournament last weekend. For judo. She's been practicing ever since she was little. She's really good at it now too. She's a fantastic athlete all-around ... and judo's her best sport.

Anyway, every time somebody wins a judo match, they advance to the next stage of the competition. That's how these tournaments work.

They started with over a hundred athletes all competing for the main prize. A giant trophy. Taller than my father! And my big sister kept winning her matches. She kept beating the other girls.

And ... kept advancing in the competition.

Before you knew it, there were only four girls left in the whole contest. Four girls out of one hundred. My sister and three others. Two semi-final matches ... and then one final match to decide the big winner.

But one of those other girls won this same tournament last year ... and the year before. So everybody expected that same girl to win again.

Everybody except me and my parents. Because we know how dedicated my big sister is. So we were very happy ... when she won the whole tournament ... but we weren't very surprised!

And now we have to figure out where the heck we're going to put that big, giant trophy! It's ginormous! It won't even fit in my sister's room. It's so big ... it's got its own zip code! I could probably take a bath inside that thing!

But I won't. Because my sister's really, really good at judo. Obviously!

I Love to Read!

My baby sister is hilarious. She's only five years old, but she sat herself down at my father's desk the other day and started hitting letters on his computer. Real fast too.

I asked what she was doing, and she said she was writing a book. So I asked what her book was about and she said – "*I don't know ... I can't read yet!*"

But my little sister has the right idea! Better than a lot of older kids. Nobody wants to read anymore. My teacher even got mad at our class. Because we were supposed to read a book, but everybody wanted to watch the movie instead. We need to read.

And I don't think it's just us kids. My dad tells a story about a famous writer who goes to a big Hollywood party. He meets a famous movie producer.

This producer says – "*I loved your last book.*"

So the writer asks – "*Oh, did you read it?*"

And the producer says – "*Well, not personally.*"

That's funny, right? But it's a good lesson too. Maybe people don't read like they used to. But I think they would really like to read more. And maybe watching good movies gives people good reasons to read all the good books that started all those good movies.

Good idea, right? Right?

Good answer!

Another Substitute Teacher

We had another substitute teacher today. That has to be the worst job on the entire planet. Maybe all the planets combined. Worst in the whole solar system.

I don't even know why anybody would want to be a substitute teacher. And some of those substitutes are real smart. Probably good teachers too.

But not in my class. They can't be good teachers when they walk into our classroom. Because every time we have a sub, my class goes crazy. The kids start acting up. Acting wild. Like ... I don't know ... like a bunch of little pirates or gremlins or something.

They're not like that with our regular teacher. So why do they behave so badly with a sub? I guess it's because they're not afraid. They think the substitute can't get them in trouble ... can't do anything to them.

But if they don't pay attention, the substitute can't do anything *for them* either. The substitute can't teach our class the stuff our regular teacher left for us ... on her desk.

And that's really a shame. It's lose-lose for everybody. Because now we all got behind in our classwork. And our regular teacher's out sick. And this nice stranger ... who came to work at our school for just one day ... has been totally disrespected.

Not Cool

Attention, class! I gotta tell you something most people won't. Most people won't tell you because it's not cool. Well, I don't wanna be cool. I wanna be the opposite of cool. I wanna be warm. I wanna be friendly and tell you something that's gonna help you.

Don't smoke. Don't start. And if you already started ... then stop.

People say it's hard to stop. It's not. This is how you do it. Stop putting cigarettes in your mouth and stop lighting them.

It's simple. Might not be easy, but it's simple.

Too much abuse has gone on for too long. Too many people got sick and died because of stupid cigarettes.

When grown-ups go to the doctor, what's the first thing they ask? Correct! *"Do you smoke?"* Always answer, "No!" Don't smoke. If your mom and dad smoke – or your uncle or your grandpa – then have this conversation with them too. We have to help! Sometimes, the kid has to be the adult. When the adults keep messing up.

Warning! They might get mad at you. They won't think you're cool. And you won't be cool. You'll be warm. Warm and friendly and helpful. You'll be doing the best thing you can do for a loved one. Or a friend. Or a stranger.

Try it and see what happens. You might even save someone's life. Someday, they'll thank you for it. Just ... probably not today.

Act Your Age ... Not Your Shoe Size!

Can I tell you something? You know what really bugs me?
People are always trying to be something they're not. Nobody wants to be themselves any more. People don't even act their real age. Young kids want to be older. Older people want to be younger. Like my grandmother, for example.

She's a real sweet lady. She's getting up there in years now. But she doesn't even want to accept that she's getting older. But she is! When she was my age, Captain Crunch was still in the Cub Scouts.

My grandmother asked where she could get a cool, young-looking haircut. So she could look real young. Like my mom. So Grandma went to Mom's place. Got her hair cut real short just like my mother. Now Grandma doesn't look like an old lady anymore. Now she looks like an old man!

She would be much better off just trying to be herself. Because we all think herself is perfect! We love the way she is! But she keeps trying to be something she's not. She's always trying to be younger!

And young kids in my school try to act older! Some of them steal cigarettes from their parents! Cigarettes?! That won't make them more grown-up. Just smellier!

Look, I'm just a kid ... and I don't understand everything about everything. But I think young people and old people should just be themselves. People should act the way nature intended.

Act the way nature made you. Because nature made you just right. Nature made you perfect.

Something To Think About ...

Did you ever hear that old joke about Thomas Edison? This one is so old it has whiskers. Thomas Edison said to his wife – "*I have good news and bad news. The good news is I invented the light bulb. The bad news is I can't get it to ring.*"

Pretty funny, right? I thought it was funny. Good thing he invented the light bulb too. If he didn't ... we'd never know when cartoon characters have a good idea.

I know, I know. That's another joke.

But why would Thomas Edison try to make the light bulb ring? He wouldn't. He's way too smart. But most of us make that mistake. We try to use the right thing ... but in the wrong way.

You can't make a light bulb ring. You can't make a cat bark. And you can't do something bad ... and then expect it to turn out good.

We should always try our best. And do the right thing in the right way. And always be willing to learn.

It's like my grandpa says ... whenever he thinks I'm acting like I know everything.

Grandpa says – "*Just when they think they've got all the answers ... I change the questions!*"

Grandpas are like that. They make you laugh ... and also give you good ideas to think about. And help you learn. I think grandpas are a lot like Thomas Edison.

The Art Museum

I went to the best place last week. My Uncle Adam and my Aunt Judith took me to an art museum. It was really beautiful. One of the nicest places I ever visited. Like a little mini-vacation.

Paintings and statues by famous artists from all over the world.

My favorite was by this lady from another country. Her name is Orlee. I never even heard that name before. I thought her name was so unique. Orlee Hadari. Her paintings were so strong and so interesting. Like nothing I ever saw before. They were unique too – like her name. You can tell just by looking at her work that she's a deep thinker.

And it made me start thinking deeper too.

What gives an artist the idea to do a beautiful painting? Where does that idea come from? Where does any idea come from? For a painting, a sculpture, a drawing. Even literature, like a poem, a story, or a book.

Then it hit me. Creative ideas are all around us. One idea leads to another and then another.

If this lady's painting in a museum can make me think about where ideas come from ... maybe my ideas can give someone else an idea for something creative too.

And that means ... ideas are all connected ... and maybe all of us are connected in the same way. That's thinking deeper too, right? And that's definitely a good thing.

Little Magic Donut Seeds

Do you ever eat my favorite cereal? The one shaped like an "O?" Full of vitamins. I could eat those delicious little "O's" for breakfast, lunch, and dinner. All day, every day, and twice on Sundays. Even for Thanksgiving dinner. Christmas dinner too. It's been my favorite cereal for a long, long time now. But I'm embarrassed to say it wasn't always that way.

When I was little, I would never touch them. My mom didn't understand why. My brothers and sisters loved them so much. You always see moms and dads giving their kids those little "O's" for snack time. They carry them around for their kids in little plastic bags when they go out. Right? You've seen that.

So my grandma told me — *"Those O's are not really Cereal O's. They're actually little magic donut seeds. When you eat a big bowl of those happy, cheery O's, they'll grow into hundreds of little baby donuts inside your tummy."*

My beautiful grandmother ... may she rest in peace ... who always found a way to help me do the right thing ... and always found a funny way to make a joke about it. I miss her so much. I miss her every day. I think about her every morning when I eat those "O's."

And plant those little magic donut seeds like my beautiful grandma taught me how to do.

The Spaghetti Strainer

I want to be good. Honest, I do. I'm nice to people. I try to do all my homework.

But yesterday was a very hard day. Some of the older kids were outside fighting and making a lot of noise. Our next-door neighbor was playing his music real loud again. Mom and Dad were yelling and screaming at each other too.

I tried and I tried and I tried, but I couldn't concentrate on my homework. I was almost ready to give up. Then I looked up from the table and saw the spaghetti strainer. That thing that separates the spaghetti we want from the hot water we don't want.

And I thought – *"Let me pretend I have one of those in my brain."*

Our ears might hear noise from outside – but we don't have to listen to all of it. Strain that out with your spaghetti strainer. Strain out all the stuff you don't want to allow into your head. It can't get in there if you don't let it. Don't invite it in. Only listen to the good information from now on.

Like that friendly, happy little voice from somewhere deep down inside ... that always tells you to be good.

Green Bananas

Did I ever tell you about my Uncle Louie? Uncle Louie always tries to save money. And that's a good thing. But sometimes a person can take that too far.

Like with food. Sometimes Uncle Louie buys food at the dollar store – instead of the regular supermarket. And he bought a bunch of green bananas. They were still green ... so that means not ripe. Not ready to eat yet. But that's okay. Mom buys green bananas from the supermarket too sometimes.

Except Uncle Louie's green bananas never turned yellow. They stayed green! What's that all about?! That was like a month ago ... and they're still green!

So Uncle Louie took them back to the store ... but they said no returns allowed on bananas. Non-refundable. Then Uncle Louie really went bananas. Started yelling and screaming in the store because he wanted his dollar back. So security told him he had to get out. And the Mister Manager Man said he can never, ever come back to this store again.

Now Uncle Louie only buys regular yellow bananas in the regular, normal store. Like regular, normal people. Because the dollar store made a monkey out of my uncle. I guess sometimes ... you really do get what you pay for.

Grown-Ups Are Busy!

Grown-ups are so busy these days! My mom's super busy. She always tries to multi-task. Do two things at once. Even when she's cooking. When she makes pancakes, she puts popcorn in the batter so they flip over by themselves!

My dad's busy too. He has to make a lot of phone calls for his work. Always talking on the phone, While he's driving, while he's exercising ... and every night when we're eating dinner. Sometimes I even hear him talking on his phone in the bathroom! Seriously, Dad?! Don't you want both hands free?!

Grandma and Grandpa are busy too. They have part-time jobs. They volunteer at the museum. And take Zumba classes on the weekend.

They make jokes about it. They say they put carbon paper between the sheets to double up on their sleep. All the older people laugh when they say that.

The younger people just ask – "*What the heck is carbon paper?*" But my grandparents are usually too busy to explain.

Look, I know grown-ups don't like to listen to us kids. But I think they all need to slow down. Relax. Take a chill pill. Stop and smell the roses.

You don't have to google "roses." You don't have to find the best roses website or app. Just stop and smell them. Those roses will help you relax. Those roses always know what to do.

Chewable Vitamins

My mom brought home these chewable vitamins. Fruit-flavored, you know? All different colors. Pretty tasty too. I think they make 'em tasty so the kids wanna eat 'em. Makes sense, right? Right.

I would eat one in the morning before school. Never really thought about it. Just popped one in my mouth. Chewed it up on the way to the bus stop. Pretty tasty. Just like bubble gum.

Then one day ... I thought about it. Why do these little bubble gum vitamins taste so good? So I sat down and read the bottle. You know what the first ingredient was? Sugar! Sugar?!

Why is sugar the main ingredient in a vitamin? That doesn't even make any kind of sense. Sugar should be the last thing anybody would want to put inside a vitamin. But these people put it in first. First ingredient. That means there's more sugar in there than anything else. More sugar than any other ingredient. What the heck kind of vitamin is that?!

Sure, there's some vitamins in there too. Lower down on the list. But this is more like a bottle of candy than a bottle of vitamins.

Think about the healthiest people you ever saw. The best athletes on TV. Got a funny feeling they're not taking these fruit-flavored, bubble gum vitamins. Got a funny feeling they're taking real vitamins. Got a funny feeling I should take real vitamins too.

Getting a Little Too Skinny

I'm getting a little worried about my Cousin Susie. She was always a little bit heavy. Just a little. Not too much.

She used to eat and eat and eat. And eat and eat and eat. Then eat some more. A lot of junk food too. So ... of course, she got a little heavy. Just a little. Not too much.

Well ... Cousin Susie finally decided to do something about it. In a big, big way. She made some *major changes* in her life. She stopped drinking sodas. Stopped eating desserts. Those used to be her favorites. She stopped eating anything after seven o'clock in the evening. She started drinking tons of water too. She even joined a gym.

But a person can go too far, don't you think? I sure do. Now I think she's getting too skinny! She's so skinny ... when she turns sideways you can't even see her! She's so skinny ... she has to run back and forth in the shower just to get wet! She's so skinny ... for Halloween she put on a blue bodysuit, a big white hat, and big, white, fluffy slippers. She went as a Q-tip!

Okay, I'm exaggerating now. But not by much. Getting too skinny is no joke, you know. I think it's worse than getting too heavy.

I think we all need a little balance in our lives. Not too heavy. Not too skinny. Kinda like Goldilocks. Goldilocks had the right idea. Maybe somewhere in the middle is just about right.

Addition and Subtraction

A lot of kids in my school have a problem with math. When are they ever going to use it? Never! They don't think they'll ever use it. Not even addition and subtraction.

But if you think about it, we use math all the time. We always have to add good stuff to our lives. And subtract bad things at the same time.

Multiplication and division too. When we find something good in our lives ... something that works well ... we should try to multiply it. Times two. Times three if we can. That way, we'll have more of the good things ... more good things that are similar to the good things we already have.

And if we have something bad ... some problem ... we can use division to divide it. The way to do that is by telling somebody we have a problem.

A parent. A teacher. A counselor. Somebody.

That way, we're never dealing with a bad problem all by ourselves. We're dividing it by two. Even dividing it by three if we can.

And that's how we use the beautiful science of math, ladies and gentlemen. Addition and multiplication for all the good stuff. Subtraction and division for all the bad stuff. And that all adds up to a very good plan of action for all us kids.

The Teacher's Pet

These two kids in my class always try to be the teacher's pet. They try to be teacher's pet every day. I never liked the idea of kids acting that way. And I never liked the idea of a teacher's pet.

These kids act real nice in class. They volunteer. They give out the books. They collect all the papers. They help straighten up the room before we leave for the day.

And that's good. Those are good things. It's good to do good things. Of course it is.

The only problem is ... these kids just do good things when they're in class. When our teacher is watching. After school ... or in the hallway ... or on the bus going home ... these same kids don't act the same. They don't act so nice when the teacher's not watching. In fact, they act worse than mostly anybody else ... when it's just us kids who are around.

That's why I don't like the idea of a teacher's pet. Nobody should be the teacher's pet. A real pet should be a pet all the time. Not part of the time.

Like your pet at home. Your dog is a dog all the time. He's not a dog with you and an armadillo when he's alone with all his doggie friends. So I think our teacher should train these teacher's pets correctly ... like you'd train a real pet. Maybe by rolling up their homework papers and rapping them on the nose. Because it doesn't hurt, but it makes a loud obnoxious noise. Kinda like the loud, obnoxious noise they make in the hall and on the bus!

Distracted and Double Parked

Help! I need your advice. I have a hard time asking for help. But I need some serious grown-up advice on this one.

Because it's a subject I know nothing about. It has to do with driving. Unfortunately, I think a lot of grown-ups don't know anything about it either.

At least I've got an excuse. I can't start driving for another six years. Maybe sooner if I take Drivers' Ed. But my parents should probably take Drivers' Ed with me. Maybe the driving school will give us a family discount.

Every time I'm in the car with my parents, I get scared out of my mind.

My mom's distracted! She drinks coffee, puts on make-up, and talks non-stop on the phone. Sometimes she has the phone in one hand, her coffee cup in the other hand, and holds the steering wheel with her knee.

Believe it or not, my's dad worse! He makes mistakes when the car's not even moving. He double-parks all the time. When he goes back to his car, there's usually a ticket. And then he starts complaining ... and he stuffs that ticket into the glove department with all the other tickets. Says he'll take care of them later. Some day he'll go back to the car and there'll be no car ... just tickets.

And there'll be no later. Because you just can't keep doing stuff like that!

What happened to following the rules?! And why am I the one pointing this out? I'm just a kid! But sometimes a kid has a fresh perspective. Sometimes a kid has to be the adult in the room.

And I am that adult.

Little People

I can still remember the first time I ever saw a little person. I was with my dad at the grocery store. Dad told me that's what they prefer to be called. *Little people.* You have to say *Little People.* They used to call them either midgets or dwarves. But I think that's considered disrespectful now.

Anyway, this was a grown man with gray hair, moustache, and a beard ... except he was the exact same height as me. I never saw anybody who looked like that before ... and I guess I was confused. And I guess I was staring. And I guess that's also disrespectful.

And then I did something totally rude. But not on purpose. I asked my dad out loud – *"What kind of a kid is that?"*

My dad didn't know what to say. And then there was a long pause. I think it's what you call one of those uncomfortable pauses. And then this man ... this little person answers back – *"I don't know. What kind of a kid are you?"*

And I didn't know what to say. I had really offended him. My dad took me by the hand and we walked away. Dad still didn't know what to say ... and now he was really embarrassed. So we were out of there. Fast. Dad explained it all to me later.

And it made me think ... how many times do we all talk before thinking? That's backwards. It has to be the opposite. We should always think before talking. There's a lot of things out there we don't understand. So we always need more thinking.

But we don't always need more talking.

Hitting the Gym

I don't understand my father. I don't understand how he does it. He does so much.

He puts us all to sleep at night. Sometimes he helps Mom check our homework after dinner. Homework is usually Mom's job, not Dad's. But he helps.

Dad works really long hours at his job. He even gets up early so he can go to the gym for an hour before work. When the doctor told him he had to lose weight, he started hitting the gym right away. He didn't waste time. He's taken off a few pounds already. I'm really proud of him, because that's not so easy for grown-ups when they get older.

I don't even know how he goes to the gym that early. Honestly, I get tired when I go to gym class in the middle of the day.

And on the weekends, when everybody else's father is on the couch watching sports ... he goes over to his parents' house to help them with all their stuff. He never complains, either. He does everything with a big smile on his face.

I don't even know when he sleeps. I kinda wish he snored, so I could hear him at night. Just so I know he's okay.

I know they say dads are supposed to be the heads of the household. They're supposed to take care of everybody. But sometimes I have to wonder ... who's taking care of them?

Give Me. Get Me. Buy Me. Take Me.

You know there are kids in my class who are so spoiled. Spoiled rotten. They're always asking for stuff. Driving their parents crazy too. Give me. Get me. Buy me. Take me.

Give me more dessert. Get me the new sneakers. Buy me the new game. Take me to the mall. Their parents do everything for them. Everything they ask. And their mothers and fathers look so stressed. I don't even know how they do it. My parents would never let me get away with acting like that.

Doesn't matter, because I wouldn't want to behave that way. That's not me. Pushy. Bossy. It's not right. It's like being a bully. Sounds funny, saying kids are bullying their parents ... but that's what it's like when you really think about it. Even if you don't think about it. Kids telling their parents what to do? It's definitely a type of bullying.

I think those parents want to make everything easy for their kids. Make everything nice. Maybe because things were difficult for them when they were little.

But that's the wrong way to help. You have to let people do things for themselves. Yes! Even kids have to do that! That's how we learn!

And kids have to learn that the answer is not always "yes." I'm a kid and I'm just telling you because it's the truth. Give me? Get me? Buy me? Take me? No, thank you.

What Kind of a Store?

Can you please explain something to me? Something I never understood – ever since I was a little kid.

Why do they have liquor stores? No, I understand, of course. They have them to sell liquor. But why do we need a whole store just for that?! Doesn't make any kind of sense. When I go to the supermarket with my mom and dad, there's one whole aisle for beers and wines and all kinds of other drinking stuff. One big aisle full of it. Both sides of the aisle too. Like a million, billion different kinds. Isn't that enough?

Why do they need a whole, separate store to sell alcoholic liquor by itself? So they can have even more different choices that supermarkets don't have? Seriously?! All those bottles in the supermarket are not enough? How much alcohol do people need to drink? How drunk do people need to get?

Don't answer that question. I don't want to know. Because there's already a million kinds my parents never heard of in the regular supermarket. Millions of different brands. If people want to try a new kind of alcohol every day, they'll never run out of choices in a whole year.

So I don't think you need a whole, separate store for alcohol. Maybe I'll think differently when I'm all grown-up. When I'm legal age. When I'm allowed to drink. But I sure hope not.

The Beautiful Nurse from El Salvador

We met this lady at church. Yaneth is her name. That's Janet in Spanish. She's so beautiful everyone stares. I guess that's the first thing they notice.

But talk with her ... and you'll see all the wonderful qualities beneath the surface. There's so very much more to this woman than meets the eye. Her personal story is inspiring. She's from El Salvador. I didn't even know where that was. So I looked it up. Small country in Central America. They had a lot of problems with earthquakes and volcanos. And a long, terrible civil war ... that hurt so many people.

This lady worked as a nurse. The beautiful nurse from El Salvador. She helped so many people in emergency situations. Saved thousands of lives. Delivered hundreds of babies. And one rainy night ... at two o'clock in the morning ... a bus crashed in the mountains. Yaneth took care of sixty people injured in the wreck – with only one other nurse working beside her all through the night.

Her mother says when she was little ... she used to give injections to her dolls. She was dreaming about becoming a nurse and helping others ... even as a little girl. She always cared. That means ... nursing is her true calling in life. She's living on purpose. Fulfilling her destiny. Doing what she was truly meant to do.

With an amazing attitude. Always smiling. Happy, warm, sweet, kind, and friendly. Treats everyone so nice. But I can't help thinking ... how many people just look ... and stare? And only talk about how beautiful she is.

When you only notice what's pretty on the outside ... beauty that's skin deep ... you don't see a complete person. You miss the real person inside. In this case, you miss something special ... someone special. You miss the very, very best ... of the beautiful nurse from El Salvador.

The Texting Team

Did you ever notice how some kids are texting all the time? Did you ever notice?! Yeah, right! How can you not notice! Some kids text all the time. More than they talk. And the kids in my school do it more than anyone I ever saw! Anyone on this whole, entire planet.

And they never even look at you when you're talking to them. That used to bother me, but now it doesn't even bother me at all.

You know why? I'll tell you. I invented a solution to all that pollution.

I think our school should start a texting team. Right. Like our basketball team or soccer team. Just exactly like that.

My math teacher can be our coach. Nobody knows more about texting than her! She's probably overqualified. She's an amazing lady. She can text with one hand, write on the board with the other, and still keep yelling at the kids in the back row.

She could really whip the Texters into shape. The Texting Team can practice in the library after school. We could travel to other schools and challenge their best texters. See who has the fastest thumbs.

The school district can start its own league. Every school sends their best texting talent. Winners go to the state championships. Maybe win a giant trophy for their school ... a big, giant championship trophy shaped like a cell phone.

Absolutely, Positively The Last Time

D id you ever hear somebody say – *"This is the last time!"*

The last time I mess up on a test. Last time I miss a homework assignment. Last time I tease my little brother.

Those ideas sound good. But we have to really do what we say. We have to make sure it's the last time. To do that, we have to make decisions. We have to make up our minds to change. We have to decide to act differently.

How? How can we do that? We have to change how we think. Pretend you're making a promise to yourself. A promise to be a different kind of human being from now on.

If you make a promise to another person, you should keep it. So make believe this is a really important promise you make to another person. And make it just as important to keep a promise you make to yourself.

Always keep your word. That's how we stop making bad decisions.

Keep the promise when you say – *"This is the last time!"*

Because if we don't make sure it's the last time ... then it's never really the last time. It's just the last time before the next time.

Afterword

One of the very best ways to learn any new subject is to try teaching and explaining it to someone else.

If you're a young actor who feels very comfortable performing scenes and monologues – and always gets good, solid feedback from your teachers – then I have a suggestion for you. Try helping an acting student who isn't as advanced as you are. Try coaching someone who has not yet developed your level of skill and confidence in the performing arts.

Acting is not as easy as it looks on television. Acting is not for everyone, and some people who want to become actors may have to overcome a little shyness or insecurity at first. If you can help another young actor practice monologues – and become more comfortable and confident on stage and screen – you'll be doing something terrific for that other person.

In the process, you'll also be doing something terrific for yourself.

About Sharon Garrison

A proud member of SAG-AFTRA and AEA, Sharon Garrison is an actor, director, coach, and short film producer. She holds undergraduate and graduate degrees from Texas Christian University. She earned her B.F.A. in Theatre/Television and her M.S. in Media Studies. A Certified Teacher in Texas (Drama K-12), she has taught in the Dallas Independent School District and many professional actor training programs. She has taught college classes at Texas Christian University, Texas Woman's University, and Tarrant County College.

Her production company, Velvet Ribbon Entertainment, is dedicated to producing short films and coaching actors' auditions for regional and national productions. Sharon serves on the Dallas-Fort Worth SAG-AFTRA Board and chairs their Conservatory committee. She has performed on stage in dozens of professional theaters, most notably Circle Theatre, Stage West, Theatre Three, Casa Mañana, Le Petite Theatre du Vieux Carre, and dinner theater tours throughout the United States.

She now focuses on film and television work, and has booked recurring roles on three television series. She played Mrs. Barnes in *Sordid Lives: The Series*; Martha in the NBC drama *Game of Silence*, and Judge Amelia Sanders in Lifetime's popular *Drop Dead Diva*.

Additional TV credits include *Preacher* (AMC), *Claws* (TNT), *American Horror Story* (FX) and *Common Law* (USA). She has worked on large scale studio feature films and independent film projects all across the United States. Most recently released is the award winning *Bomb City*, available On Demand and in select markets. She also recently appeared in *A Very Sordid Wedding* for director Del Shores. Studio pictures include the Warner Brothers feature, *Midnight Special*, directed by Jeff Nichols, and *Pitch Perfect 2*, directed by Elizabeth Banks.

Sharon attributes her active and successful career to developing a close-knit community of industry professionals around her — and taking time to nurture strong, effective working relationships with her amazing regional talent agents, *Linda McAlister Talent* and *Landrum Arts LA*.

About Mike Kimmel

Mike Kimmel is a former pro wrestler and circus magician. Nowadays, he works as a film, television, stage, and commercial actor and acting coach. He is a twenty-plus year member of SAG-AFTRA with extensive experience in both the New York and Los Angeles markets. He has worked with directors Francis Ford Coppola, Robert Townsend, Craig Shapiro, and Christopher Cain among many others. TV credits include *Game of Silence, Zoo, Treme, In Plain Sight, Cold Case, Breakout Kings, Memphis Beat, Buffy The Vampire Slayer*, and *The Oprah Winfrey Show*. He was a regular sketch comedy player on *The Tonight Show*, performing live on stage and in pre-taped segments with Jay Leno for eleven years.

Mike has appeared in dozens of theatrical plays on both coasts, including Radio City Music Hall, Equity Library Theater, Stella Adler Theater, Double Image Theater, The Village Gate, and Theater at the Improv. He trained with Michael Shurtleff, William Hickey, Ralph Marrero, Gloria Maddox, Harold Sylvester, Wendy Davis, Amy Hunter, Bob Collier, and Stuart Robinson. He holds a B.A. from Brandeis University and an M.A. from California State University.

He has taught at Upper Iowa University, University of New Orleans, University of Phoenix, Glendale Community College, Nunez Community College, Delgado Community College, and in the Los Angeles, Beverly Hills, and Burbank, California public school districts. He is a two-time past president of New Orleans Toastmasters, the public speaking organization, and often serves as an international speech contest judge. Mike has written and collaborated on numerous scripts for stage and screen. *In Lincoln's Footsteps*, his full-length historical drama on Presidents Lincoln and Garfield, was a 2013 semi-finalist in the National Playwrights Conference at the Eugene O'Neill Theater Center. He is the 2014 recipient of the Excellence in Teaching Award from Upper Iowa University.

Mike is a full voting member of the National Academy of Television Arts and Sciences, the organization that produces the Emmy Awards. He is the author of *Scenes for Teens, Monologues for Teens*, and *Acting Scenes for Kids and Tweens*.

"Thought is the most vital and powerful thing in the entire universe. All the good and evil in the world is the result of right or wrong thinking and each of us is contributing something to the sum total one way or the other every second."

– Mary Pickford

Made in the USA
San Bernardino, CA
10 July 2020